sumatra
tawar

café life
NEW YORK

An Insider's Guide to the City's Neighborhood Cafés

Written by Sandy Miller
Photography by Juliana Spear

First published in 2008 by

INTERLINK BOOKS
An imprint of Interlink Publishing Group, Inc.
46 Crosby Street, Northampton, Massachusetts 01060
www.interlinkbooks.com

Text copyright © Sandy Miller 2008
Photography copyright © Juliana Spear 2008
Design copyright © Interlink Publishing 2008
Map by Jacob Shemkovitz

Library of Congress Cataloging-in-Publication Data
Miller, Sandy.
 Café life New York : an insiders guide to the city's
neighborhood cafes/by Sandy Miller; photography by
Juliana Spear.
     p. cm.
 ISBN-13: 978-1-56656-703-9 (pbk.)
1. Coffeehouses—New York (State)—New York—
Guidebooks. 2. New York (N.Y.)—Social life and customs.
3. New York (N.Y.)—Guidebooks. I. Spear, Juliana. II. Title.
TX907.3.N72M45 2008
647.95747'1—dc22

                                    2007031864

Printed and bound in China

To request our 40-page full-color catalog, please visit our
website at: www.interlinkbooks.com, call us toll-free at:
1-800-238-LINK, or write to us at: Interlink Publishing,
46 Crosby Street, Northampton, MA 01060

The only person who partakes of the most essential charm of this splendid coffeehouse is he who wants nothing there but to be there. Purposeless sanctifies the stay.
—Alfred Polgar, "Theory of the Café Central"

CONTENTS

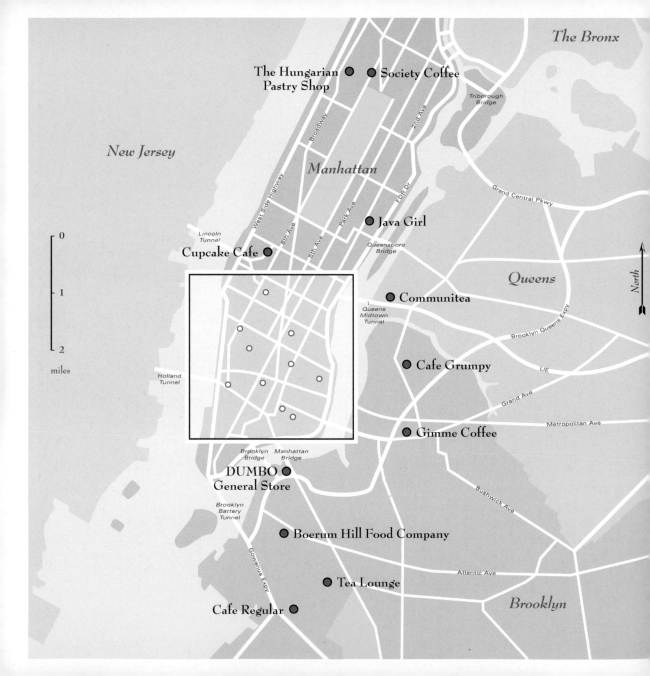

The Bronx

New Jersey

The Hungarian Pastry Shop

Society Coffee

Triborough Bridge

Manhattan

Broadway

2nd Ave

Grand Central Pkwy

West Side Highway

FDR Dr

Lincoln Tunnel

Park Ave

Java Girl

8th Ave

5th Ave

Queensboro Bridge

Cupcake Cafe

Queens

0

Communitea

1

Queens Midtown Tunnel

Brooklyn Queens Expy

2

Cafe Grumpy

LIE

miles

Holland Tunnel

Grand Ave

Metropolitan Ave

Gimme Coffee

North

Brooklyn Bridge

Manhattan Bridge

DUMBO General Store

Bushwick Ave

Brooklyn Battery Tunnel

Boerum Hill Food Company

Gowanus Expy

Atlantic Ave

Tea Lounge

Cafe Regular

Brooklyn

0

¼

½

miles

West Side Hwy

9th Ave

34th St

FDR Dr

Chelsea

8th Ave

7th Ave

23rd St

Broadway

Park Ave

3rd Ave

2nd Ave

W 14th St

**Gramercy /
Union Square**

● Antique Cafe

● Grounded
Organic Coffee & Tea House

● 71 Irving Place
Coffee & Tea Bar

● Joe
The Art of Coffee

E 14th St

1st Ave

West Village

W Houston St

Broadway

Lafayette St

Bowery

● Mudspot

Avenue C

East Village

Holland Tunnel

6th Ave

● Ninth Street
Espresso

Kiva Cafe ●

SoHo

● Housing Works
Used Book Cafe

Hudson St

Canal St

E Houston St

Pitt St

Lower East Side

Delancey St

88 Orchard ●

Allen St

Manhattan Br

● **Full City Coffee**

FDR Dr

Williamsburg Br

North

INTRODUCTION

*B*efore one can write about café life, one must first define "café," and in New York that can be a challenge. The names of places claiming the word "café" encompass bistros, restaurants, bakeries, pizzerias, lounges, wine bars, and more. The corner deli puts two tables out on the sidewalk, and presto!—"café seating." A sign outside an establishment on the Upper West Side says "Bakery, Restaurant, Café." A certain "café" on Manhattan's Upper East Side has a sign in front that announces "Café: Pizza, Bakery, Sushi, Carving Board, Grill, Coffee Bar." And in the East Village a sign for a tattoo parlor reads: "Tattoos and Cappuccino." You see the problem.

Café Life New York focuses on cafés—no matter what they call themselves—that function mainly as gathering places with coffee and/or tea as the central offering. They serve pastries and baked goods that go with the drinks, and maybe light fare as well, but food, whether fast or slow, is not the raison d'etre. These cafés beckon the patron who has come to stay awhile, often a long while—order a single cup of coffee, and you are welcome to stay as long as you wish. High turnover is not the goal. Rather, the primary purpose is to provide a "third place"—beyond home and work. Given the city's cramped quarters, this is often a godsend.

All of the cafés in this book are neighborhood cafés. Mostly located in residential neighborhoods, usually on less traveled, lower-rent streets, they are known primarily to locals who loyally support their beloved little neighborhood places. They are not dessert cafés, date cafés, or tourist attractions. They are not coffee-to-go, take-it-on-the-run espresso bars. Nor are they parts of chains; they are independently owned labors of love. The personalities of the owners loom large and their involvement in the daily workings of the café is pervasive. These places have a regular clientele for whom a visit to the café is an integral part of their daily routine, and the social interactions and relations that result can shape their lives. Call it café life.

These cafés are the spiritual descendants of the city's earliest cafés. Café life in New York did not begin in 1994 when a certain Seattle-based chain opened its first New York location at Broadway and 87th Street on Manhattan's Upper West Side. In fact, the first coffeehouse (used here and throughout this book synonymously with café) in the city was established in 1696, on Broadway between what is now Liberty and Cedar Streets, just north of Trinity Church in the financial district. (Boston claims America's very first coffeehouse [1670], but New York was a close second.)

Started by an Englishman who was inspired by the coffeehouses that proliferated in England from the 1650s until the early 1800s, that first New York coffeehouse, like its British model, was meant to be an egalitarian place where citizens of all classes could come and be welcomed. It was to be a place where people of diverse backgrounds and interests could gather in a convivial atmosphere to socialize, to read newspapers, to discuss politics, to conduct business—or to be alone, if one wished. And, of course, to drink coffee—the perfect drink, then and now, for the city that never sleeps.

The original spirit of New York's first coffeehouse persists. Even the way chairs were arranged in the early coffeehouses—to encourage strangers to talk to strangers—or the use of communal tables toward that same end, can be found in the city's cafés today. The defining features of the early coffeehouses sound decidedly contemporary—just add laptops.

Café Life New York is organized by neighborhood and includes most every Manhattan neighborhood—excluding Midtown. Aside from not really being a neighborhood, rents there preclude the sort of café otherwise included. After an introduction to the neighborhood, the pieces on the chosen cafés share the point of view of its owners as well as its patrons. Each section ends with a Short Cups listing of other cafés in that neighborhood worthy of visiting.

To the extent that these cafés reflect the neighborhood in which they are located, the neighborhoods also reflect the character and demographic of its cafés. To know a café is to know a neighborhood. Consider *Café Life New York*, then, as offering both cafés *and* neighborhoods—a double treat. That is, as you may find yourself saying at a café counter, *un doppio*. Enjoy!

· 1 ·

LOWER EAST SIDE

Though its exact boundaries are a matter of opinion, this part of Manhattan includes the area south of East Houston Street from the East River over to ever-expanding Chinatown on the south and west. Known for its working-class, immigrant history, the Lower East Side is identified in the public imagination as the "Jewish Lower East Side," though its Jewish population and commercial establishments have dwindled. The neighborhood's newer "immigrants" include Asians, hipsters, artists, young professionals, and a new wave of observant Jews. Expect to see vendors of kosher pickles and women's undergarments next door to sushi bars and upscale clothing boutiques, on the same block as a yeshiva day school, a Chinese cybercafé, and a mosque.

88 Orchard

**88 Orchard Street
(between Broome
and Grand Streets)
(212) 228-8880
Open 7:30AM–8PM
Mon to Fri
8:30AM–8PM Sat & Sun
Subway: F to Delancey;
J, M, Z, to Essex**

Few Manhattan neighborhoods have changed as rapidly or as dramatically as the Lower East Side. 88 Orchard, a bright, cozy two-level café with wraparound front windows (and one uniquely New York City window that looks out onto an air shaft) was a harbinger of that change.

"We were the new kid on the block when we opened," says Erica Harrison, one half of the sister duo (Tara Katz is the other) who started 88 Orchard in what had been a brass bed store. "That was 2003. And when we opened," she says, "we were among the very few places in the neighborhood where you could get a quick cup of coffee. There certainly was no Starbucks here on the Lower East Side yet. A lot of the old lingerie stores were still in business then. Not anymore."

Not anymore to be sure. Within a very short period of time, the lingerie shops, along with other old-time Jewish-owned businesses—mostly clothes-related and of the kind that sold goods straight from the packing box—were quickly replaced by cafés, restaurants, bakeries, vintage clothing stores, antique shops, wine bars, and the like. In just a few years' time, 88 Orchard went from new kid on the block to neighborhood fixture to elder statesman. No—stateswoman.

Ironically, the Jewish immigrant history of the neighborhood, which the sisters' family shares, was a major reason Erica and Tara located here. But that history is now mostly found in the Lower East Side Tenement Museum, half a block away at 108 Orchard. A Jewish business presence still exists, though dispersed and substantially thinned out, and Asian—Chinese mostly—and trendy businesses have taken over, serving mostly young people.

Before deciding what to do with the rest of their lives, both sisters traveled widely and lived for extended periods in different places: Seville, Spain, Israel (Erica in the north and Tara in Tel Aviv), San Francisco. Erica worked in, and ultimately managed, a new café in Melbourne, Australia. All these seemingly disparate places have vibrant café cultures.

But eventually, the sisters came back to their native New York, with an idea about working together and owning their own place. "We knew only too well the limitations of working in a place that was not your own," says Erica. "We felt New York is a great city, but it's a crazy city too—it doesn't give people a chance to stop. That's what we decided we wanted to do. Create a space where people could *stop*. Just stop.

"A real inspiration for us was our great-grandmother who ran a candy store in Crown Heights in Brooklyn… The store had been closed by the time we were born, but our great-grandmother lived until we were in our teens, so we grew up with these incredible stories about the candy store. It being this integral part of the community and she being this strong woman who ran it.

"Those are my great-grandparents in front of the candy store," she says, pointing to a black-and-white photograph that sits on the café's front bar. "We like the fact that our front door (framed-glass, double doors) is similar to the candy store's. And our chicken noodle soup is a variation of our great-grandmothers'!"

All they needed was the name. "For the longest time we didn't have one," Erica admits. "We just couldn't agree. But when it came time to file for incorporation, we

needed a d.b.a. So, we put down doing-business-as '88 Orchard,' and after awhile it just stuck. Also… as a child, Tara was infatuated with the number eight. It was her lucky number. And come to find out, in Chinese culture, eight signifies prosperity. And we had two… double prosperity! We tried to convince the phone company to give us as many eights in our phone number as possible. We have four, which makes us pretty lucky."

The interior of the café is attractive and entirely unassuming. In the renovation, they stripped the space to its original walls and ceilings as much as possible. Two levels of drop ceilings disappeared. The wrecked original pressed tin ceiling was replaced with new pressed tin, which evokes an earlier time. The exquisite vaulted brick ceiling downstairs is one of the gems of the restoration.

Downstairs, the tabletops have a floral design created out of treated copper by a local craftsperson, who also plastered the downstairs walls. Another artist, a sculptor friend of Tara and Erica, created the treated lead and copper facade of the upstairs bar. The work of local artists is up on the walls, typically changing every three months or so. Though in the case of Kevin Cyr, his work was so right for the space that it stayed up for months and months. "We became his own private gallery," says Erica. "His work gave a nice masculine balance to what some might say is a too feminine-feeling space. But what do you expect when two women design it?"

88 Orchard attracts different customers and serves diverse functions throughout the course of the day. During the morning, after the grab-a-coffee rush hour crowd, the breakfast regulars—artists, writers, fashion designers, freelancers of various sorts—settle in, many stay for hours. Some come everyday. A few come twice a day. "For certain people," says Erica, "this is their office."

Starting at lunchtime, the regulars are replaced by tourists, many from the Tenement Museum up the street. (On weekends, there are so many tourists that the locals tend not to show up.) People who work in the neighborhood, including museum staff, come in for lunch or for a coffee break later in the afternoon. These include many Chinese businessmen who work in the area, and teachers from the nearby massive Seward Park High School and a public elementary school.

As evening approaches, the regulars trickle back, until the crowd is mostly local. They come with their laptops or for a meeting and have just a glass of wine or a cup of coffee.

At any time of day, the upstairs and downstairs have different uses. While the upstairs is crowded, with about ten small tables and a small counter in front of one of the windows, the downstairs has two communal tables and is quieter and more open. Writers gravitate to the large tables and spread out. Laptop users are left alone.

There is little doubt that 88 Orchard takes their coffee seriously. "We knew that everything would revolve around it," says Erica. "So, we took our time to choose our supplier."

88 Orchard uses coffee from Irving Farm, a small batch roaster in Millerton, New York (see page 88). The Irving Farm House Blend, a smooth mix of Kenyan, Colombian, and Sumatran beans, is used for their drip coffee. An intensely flavored, single-origin Sumatra coffee is also offered, as well as a hazelnut. 88 Orchard won't put it through their own grinder. For their decaf, they use Irving Farm Estate Blend, a combination of beans from Central and South America that gives the coffee a slight mocha taste. Iced coffee, incidentally, is made with coffee ice cubes—"A lot of effort," says Erica, "but otherwise, all you get is a watered-down drink."

For their espresso, the Irving Farm French Roast, with its blend of Guatemalan, Brazilian, Sumatran, and Java beans, is the coffee of choice. All espressos are pulled as double shots on a handmade Italian Magister two-group espresso machine and made in the "European way," which means not using a spoon to pour the foam.

Perhaps as a remnant of Erica's Melbourne experience, where espresso reigned, 88 Orchard takes particular care with its espresso drinks. "You hardly saw drip coffee in Melbourne. Even little shops, the equivalent here to a bodega, would have espresso machines and serve a really excellent espresso."

"It's all about the consistency of the foam," says Erica. "There's a difference, for example, between the consistency of the foam for a cappuccino and a latte. It's smoother for a latte. We train our baristas to hear when the milk is ready... In steaming milk, you have to get a complete twirling action, and then when you hear the roar, you cut it off. If you don't cut if off at the start of the roaring sound, the milk gets too hot."

"Also," she continues, "You don't want bubbles in the foam. You want a smooth texture. If you let the air in early, it allows the bubbles to work themselves out into the foam. I don't like the hissing sound. It means air is being let in too late."

88 Orchard tries to hire baristas with experience and goes to great lengths to train all new workers. All must pass a bar test. Many on staff come from Washington and Oregon, although Erica admits their very first barista was a young woman she stole away from a Manhattan café. "I liked her drinks and I liked the way she moved," she says with a broad smile. "She was great."

Some staff can do latte art. "When they're really on their

game," claims Erica. "But what's most important is getting a great cup of coffee. If you can get a great cup of coffee that also looks pretty, well, better yet."

In addition to coffee, 88 Orchard offers teas blended by Harney & Sons (also in Millerton), soft drinks, specialty drinks such as ice-cream floats, wine, and beer. Baked goods come from local suppliers: bread from Amy's Bread, rugelach from Betsy's, other sweets from Sage American Catering. One of the vegan cookies comes from California. Otherwise everything is local, including produce from a Brooklyn market. Soups, salads, dressings, and sandwiches are made on the premises. But the slice of pickle accompanying every sandwich comes from Guss Pickles across the street, which has been around since 1910!

Erica talks about some of the highlights and quirks of 88 Orchard:

"The guy who collected other people's newspapers and then tried to sell them to our customers.

"The homeless guy who came in everyday, ordered a coke, asked for a receipt, sat down with his newspaper, and spent hours circling all the 'no's' in the paper.

"People who come in and say ours is the best cappuccino they ever had. That makes my day.

"The fact that neighborhood people leave their keys with us. Or that we receive random FedEx packages for the neighborhood.

"Watching the first snowfall of the winter. Feeling warm and toasty and looking out through all that glass at the beautiful snow falling all around as though I'm inside a snow globe. Then, having some of the regular customers help shovel.

"Watching regulars get married. Watching kids grow up. Mostly, the consistency of seeing certain people each day. And, then—noticing if you don't."

Wow. Makes you want to open a café.

Full City Coffee

**409 Grand Street
(at Clinton Street)
(212) 260-2363
Open 7AM–7:30PM
Mon to Fri
9AM–7:30PM Sat & Sun
Subway: F, J, M, Z, to
Delancey & Essex; F to East
Broadway**

Rather than heed Horace Greeley's admonition to "Go West," Natalie Krodel and Nguyen Huynh, the husband and wife proprietors of Full City Coffee, went east. Very far east. In fact, about as far east as one can go on the Lower East Side before running into East River Drive.

"I was living just a couple of blocks away," Natalie, an ex-lawyer, explains. "I felt a real sense of community here that I didn't feel where I worked for a midtown law firm. Cooperative Village [four complexes—twelve buildings and 4,500 apartments—built by trade unions as housing for working and middle-class tenants] still has many older residents. And although the buildings have been privatized, so many old-timers continue to live there and not sell their apartments that the neighborhood is somewhat resistant to upper-middle-class hegemony."

Natalie had always been "a coffee addict," and there were few places in the neighborhood to get high quality coffee (this was 2003 and before the nearby Starbucks opened), so opening a coffeehouse seemed logical. Her husband Nguyen (pronounced "win") readily placed his imprimatur on the plan.

"I went to college in Berkeley where I was introduced to café culture," says Nguyen. "Afterwards I went to graduate school at Harvard, and experienced the student cafés in Cambridge. And, as my mother reminded me, my grandmother had run a famous café in Vietnam, in the south near the coast. It had a great location on the main north–south highway, and during the war, South Vietnamese army convoys stopped there for coffee; it was a big meeting spot."

With his grandmother's memory as inspiration, giving his blessings to Natalie's idea was foreordained. One could say, owning a café was in his blood. Now, besides working as an investment banker, he does office work for Full City and helps on the "bigger issue stuff" such as licenses. Located in what must be one of Manhattan's only strip malls, in a store that had previously been a Hallmark card shop, Full City Coffee, looks from the outside like it could be located almost anywhere.

The decor is basic and mostly nondescript. But only in New York would one find such diversity of patrons: babies, octogenarians, students, local middle-class residents, neighborhood workers, Orthodox Jews, yuppies, hipsters, Asians, Latinos, and blacks. Empty out a New York City subway car and you have an idea of Full City's mix of clientele. No, we're not in Kansas, Toto.

"The diversity is wonderful," Natalie says, "but it does offer certain challenges… A number of Orthodox Jewish customers are kosher. We could not be all kosher, nor did we want to be, but we did want to make some concessions to those customers. The coffee is not a problem. It's all natural. We decided to provide some kosher pastries—the ones that are wrapped. We had to tell our staff not to unwrap them, because then they will no longer be kosher. The syrups used for flavored coffees are kosher as well. And, of course, the bagels, from Kossar's, just down the street, although we obviously cannot get them on Saturday (the Jewish Sabbath). On Saturday we get the bagels from Zabar's."

"There are age conflicts too," Natalie continues. "Many of the elderly people in the neighborhood were not used to paying $2.00 for a cup of coffee, so we had a small coffee for a dollar on the menu. Now it's $1.25. Also, many of the older customers were used to bodega coffee, which often had a burnt taste. So, they would order coffee here, add a half a cup of cold milk to it, and then complain the coffee was not hot enough!

"And we have to have a selection of music and art palatable to all age groups. Nudity would offend our older customers, and

music has to be played at a lower volume, particularly in the morning. We're stricter about what the staff can play in the morning when loud music can be more jarring… If it was left to staff, they would play their friend's garage band CD. But it wouldn't go over with many of our customers."

From the omnipresent walker to the large-type editions of books in the café's well-stocked lending library, the presence of Full City's elderly clientele is everywhere evident. Their conversations often reflect the inimitable blend of old leftist, pro-union, activist politics that once defined the Lower East Side, and whose legacy the neighborhood's old-time residents—an endangered species in highly priced and increasingly homogenized Manhattan—still continue to nurture. "With the exception of Mr. Lattman," Natalie confesses. "He's the one conservative. He once almost literally dragged Nguyen and me to a meeting of the Federalist Society!

"Here's one of our regular customers," says Natalie, pointing to a white-haired women who tucks her walker into an out-of-the-way corner. "Her name is Ruth. She's 91! Comes in every single day. Orders quiche and a scone."

As it happens, she is the "Ruth" of the mailing labels on so many of Full City's donated periodicals: *Mother Jones*, the *Nation*, the NAACP *Crisis*, *Smithsonian*, *Sierra*, *Nature Conservancy*.

No, Toto, definitely not Kansas.

Serving high quality coffee, the initial impetus for starting Full City Coffee, continues to be the central concern. "I wanted a high quality, darker roast coffee," says Natalie. "Not burnt. New York at that time lacked quality coffee. In the beginning, I was against serving food. Only pastries. There was no room for a kitchen. We just sort of backed into food. Now we offer soups, sandwiches, and quiche. At Nguyen's urging, Vietnamese sandwiches have also been added; grilled or barbecued meats, with toppings of shredded carrots, cilantro, cucumber, or daikon served on a baguette.

"After doing research, I finally chose Batdorf & Bronson in Olympia, Washington. I thought they were well above anyone else. They source their beans very strictly, which means they reject beans that don't measure up. Also, they're committed to Fair Trade and sustainable growth. A '100% Green Powered Coffee Company' is their self-description. They roast for us every week."

For its brewed coffee, Full City's house blend is the Dancing Goats

Blend. (The name pays homage to the dancing goats in the legend of how coffee was first discovered: a goatherd in Ethiopia noticed how frisky his goats became after eating the berries of a particular shrub—which, of course, turned out to be a coffee plant.) The blend, whose combination of several beans is a proprietary secret—"a fair amount of Costa Rican beans is all I can say"—results in a brew that is dark, smooth, and sweet. "It's pretty vibrant," says Natalie. "Enough, in fact, to be used for our espresso as well."

In addition to the house blend, Full City offers a single-origin coffee of the day. Among the several brewed coffees offered—Costa Rican, Kenyan, Java, Tanzanian, and Ethiopian among them—Natalie is partial to Sumatra Lake Tawar, a full-bodied coffee with a distinct fruity taste. It was recently rated one of the best coffees in the world—94 out of 100 in the *Coffee Review* buying guide. El Salvador Finca Siberia is another big, bold coffee.

The espresso drinks are made on a two-group La Marzocca espresso machine. At least once a year, the café closes and the staff spends eight hours pulling espresso shots under the guidance of a trainer from Batdorf & Bronson. "We try to be exact," says Natalie. "We grind exactly seven ounces of coffee for each espresso. Tamp down the grinds with thirty pounds of pressure. Check the integrity of the portafilter; make sure the head is dry. Time the shots. Twenty to twenty-five seconds. Not over or under-extracted. Watch the crema. Dark, toasty crema flakes. Sweet and strong. That's it."

As to latte art? "I think it's great," she says. "Kristen is pretty good at it. But so many of our customers put lids on their coffee, which makes latte art moot. It doesn't necessarily make the drink better. It's like placing a mint on a pillow in a hotel."

And don't miss Nguyen's popular sweet and peppery Vietnamese iced coffee, made with a dark French roast with chicory and condensed milk added.

As a comment on the quality of their coffee, Nguyen tells the following story. "RuPaul (the black drag queen) was in Los Angeles with a friend from the neighborhood and was upset with the coffee he was getting out there… One day RuPaul just turned to his friend and said, 'I really miss Full City Coffee!'"

Short Cups

While on the Lower East Side, consider **Cake Shop** (152 Ludlow Street at Stanton), whose café operates amid several other activities and offerings; **Ini Ani Espresso & Wine Bar** (105 Stanton Street at Ludlow); **Lotus Lounge** (35 Clinton Street at Stanton), particularly before 6 PM, after which the café becomes a bar; and **teany** (90 Rivington Street at Orchard). You might also want to dip down into Chinatown, where there are myriad teahouses and cafés, some less daunting to tourists than others, including **Green Tea Café** (45 Mott Street between Pell and Bayard)—or across into NoLita (North of Little Italy) where you'll find **Epistrophy Wine Bar & Café** (200 Mott Street between Kenmare and Spring) as well as the **Teahouse** (52 Prince Street between Lafayette and Mulberry) within the McNally Robinson bookstore.

· 2 ·

SoHo

The name SoHo, short for South of Houston, was a precursor to a host of other neighborhood acronyms, such as Tribeca (Triangle Below Canal) and DUMBO (Down Under the Manhattan Bridge Overpass). SoHo's evolution from industrial neighborhood with cheap, under-the-radar artist's quarters to one defined by expensive galleries, boutiques, and weekend visitors from New Jersey, has been a blueprint for that kind of urban development. Located between East Houston and Canal Streets, from Lafayette on the east to Varick on the west, SoHo was once called the Cast Iron District. Magnificent examples of these cast-iron facades remain. Check out, too, the marvelous wooden water tanks on building-tops—they are part of a unique New York City system of creating water pressure in tall buildings.

Housing Works
Used Book Café

**126 Crosby Street
(between Houston & Prince Streets)
(212) 334-3324
www.housingworks.org
Open 10AM–9PM Mon to Fri
12PM–7PM Sat & Sun
Subway: N, R, W to Prince; B, D, F, V to
Broadway-Lafayette; 6 to Bleecker**

*I*f you want to escape SoHo without actually leaving, head to the Housing Works Bookstore Café. Located on an old cobblestoned block (known to New Yorkers as one of the few streets where there's a chance of finding a parking spot), it manages to be exceedingly un-SoHo-like. An oasis of non-hype in the center of SoHo hip.

Occupying space that had previously been an Army–Navy store, and a manufacturing business before then, it is as down-to-earth as present-day SoHo is chichi. Not known to many New Yorkers, and virtually unknown to visitors, the unpretentious Housing Works remains hidden in plain sight.

The bookstore and café were established in 1995 to provide financial support and visibility for the programs of Housing Works, a non-profit that provides advocacy, housing, healthcare, and other services for homeless people living with AIDS and HIV. The bookstore generates revenue through the sale of donated used records and books (its collection numbers around 45,000, making it the City's second largest used bookstore after the Strand). The café raises funds through the sale of coffee and other items. Here, you can have a double latte along with a chocolate brownie without a smidgen of guilt. It's all for a good cause.

Yet don't assume anything about Housing Works Bookstore Café by virtue of its non-profit status. There is nothing bare bones or ascetic about it. The place defies assumptions and predictability. It is spectacularly grand, yet cozy and undeniably elegant, yet homey. Designed to create the feel of an old-fashioned library or bookstore—say, the wood-paneled former Scribner's on Fifth Avenue—this two-level store, of which the café is an integral part, is high-ceilinged and mahogony-paneled. It is a highly sought after space for both special events (usually literary) and film shoots.

According to Susie Lupert, who manages the store as well as the café, everyone who comes in for the first time feels like they are the first person to discover it. "The frequent reaction," she says, "is, 'Omigod, this is the most amazing place.' … And when they discover the money they're spending goes to help people—well, that brings in a whole other level of love for the place."

The café has changed a lot since Susie arrived in 2003. "When I first came here, I felt the café had been neglected… it had the feel of a second cousin. It was run by volunteers, and if a barista didn't show, the café would be closed.

"So, when I took over, the first thing I did was make a rule that it stays open no matter what (except for special events). The baristas are still volunteers, but we always remain open. We needed to be consistent. Consistent hours, staff, coffee, etc. When I came here, I had never used an espresso machine before, but I'm very good at organizing."

She admits that the bookstore rather than the café is still the space's defining feature. "It's about the bookstore," she says, "but the café is essential. Without it, the bookstore would be a completely different place. There wouldn't be as many people hanging out, enjoying themselves, taking extra time to browse. It brings more customers and makes them stay longer. And, it makes them come back!"

Though the café counter is off to the side in the back of the bookstore, big and small tables and comfy leather armchairs spill out into the store, even to the balcony. Book-buyers read in the café. Customers take their coffee into the bookstore. There are no boundaries, which makes Housing Works perhaps New York's only 10,000-square-foot-café!

In addition to the bookstore customers and many tourists (the place is written up in several tourist guides and gets huge play in Japan, where it's often cited as among the "coolest places in New York"), there are the regulars who frequent the place often and continually. By Susie's observation, they fall into four categories: Neighborhood residents, including writers, some of whom arrive each day at the same time, stay for the same duration, sit in the same chair and order the same thing. Students, mostly from nearby NYU, especially the dorm across the street, where Housing Works has installed a small satellite café (open to the NYU community only). Dealers in used, rare, and antique books who sit and drink coffee while deciding what to buy. And Housing Works' clients who come from its drug rehab center and syringe exchange program next door.

"People meet here," she says, "but it's not a place where strangers meet and talk. I can't believe how quiet it is in here sometimes. The place can be absolutely packed and yet so quiet. It often looks like a laptop convention. People doing their work in a quiet environment where they can concentrate. Where there's not a lot of talking. And where the music is not too loud."

Despite SoHo's many famous residents, this is not a hot, celebrity hangout, though it gets its share of local musicians. Before he left the neighborhood, Sonic Youth's Thurston Moore was a regular. And, of course, while shooting movies here, actors—Gabriel Byrne, Orlando Bloom, John Cusack, and Winona Ryder, to name a few—have made good use of the café.

Several episodes of *Sex and the City* have been filmed here. Recently, scenes from the movie version of the bestselling novel, *The Girl's Guide to Hunting and Fishing* by Melissa Banks, were filmed here, as was a new film by Noah Baumbach, who wrote and directed *The Squid and the Whale*.

One Friday a month, the bookstore café is taken over for a concert series. Recent performers have included Steve Earle, Jon Mayer, and Tracy Chapman.

These movie shoots and concerts generate a great amount of revenue for Housing Works' causes, but they, along with the many readings and book signings (with such authors as Michael Cunningham, Zadie Smith, Jonathan Franzen, and Jonathan Lethem), parties, and other in-store events interrupt the rhythms of the café's life, often causing it to be closed. Susie believes they may not have as many regulars as they would otherwise because of these disruptions. "To raise as much money for our good causes and at the same time run a great place," she says, "is hard. The two often conflict."

"The volunteer baristas range in age from 16 to 70," says Susie. "Some don't have a high school diploma and some have Ph.Ds. Some are former Starbucks employees and others have never even sipped a cup of coffee… Recently we hired a part-time employee, who comes from a coffeehouse background and whose job it will be to train the café's baristas and oversee quality control.

"It might be charming when a young kid sells a book by an author he or she has never heard of, but I don't think it's charming to not be able to make a great latte.

Although when customers find out the revenue from the sale of coffee is going to a good cause… they become more forgiving of the baristas."

The quality of their coffee took a quantum leap forward once the café switched to using Fair Trade, organic coffee from Gimme Coffee of Williamsburg, Brooklyn—the medium-dark roast Bolivian Blend for brewed and the French Roast, a dark Southern Italian-style blend for espresso. Dark, "like the dead of night."

"Since switching to Gimme Coffee," says Susie, "customers actually come up to us now and tell us how great the coffee is."

In addition to its brewed coffee and full line of espresso drinks, the café offers teas and soft drinks and even wine and beer. Most of its baked goods and sweets—cookies, scones, croissants, muffins, brownies—come from Eli's Bread & Bakery. At lunch, soup, salad, bread, and quiche are on the menu.

And last, but certainly not least—it sells knishes! They come from Yonah Schimmel's, the knish bakery par excellence on the Lower East Side. Think of them as Jewish turnovers, filled with potato, or mushroom and onion, or spinach, or broccoli. For the knishes alone, you have to love this place.

What fun. And all for a good cause!

Kiva Café

**229 Hudson Street
(between Broome & Canal Streets)
(212) 229-0898
www.kivacafe.com
Open 8AM–6PM Mon to Fri
Closed weekends
Subway: 1 to Canal Street**

Kiva Café is easy to miss, particularly passing in a car, which is what many people are doing here at the entrance to the Holland Tunnel. It is a small-scale place in a large-scale, fairly desolate, industrial neighborhood. Think of it as the little café that could.

Though the neighborhood is technically SoHo, this is SoHo sans boutiques and galleries. *That* SoHo is on the other side of Sixth Avenue. But the space was available, the rent affordable, and the neighborhood in desperate need of a comfortable place to buy a good cup of coffee, sit down, stay for a while, and savor it.

"I had worked in the neighborhood," says Beebe Okoye, Kiva's 30-something owner, "and realized there was no place to go for coffee besides delis or sit-down, white-tablecloth restaurants. Nothing in between. The Starbucks (a few blocks away on Sixth Avenue) had not yet opened."

Beebe, who was born in Brooklyn but raised in Arizona, worked for many years as an architect. "I was withering on the vine," she says. "I wanted to do something a little more flexible... something where I didn't have to wait so long to see results. I started to think about all the things I liked—food, art, social interaction. I thought about how I might create my own work environment; one where I could work and socialize at the same time. Opening a little café seemed like a good idea. After all, how hard could it be?"

Well, it seemed pretty hard on opening day, January 19, 2003. "It was Martin Luther King's birthday," Beebe recalls, "and everything was closed. I didn't have enough change in the drawer. This was my first cash business. I spent almost all of that first day running up and down the street trying to find change for customers! I'll never forget it. Still, I think it was symbolic that I waited until Martin Luther King's birthday to open."

Growing up in the Southwest, Beebe was familiar with kivas, structures built by Native Americans for ceremonies or social gatherings. The concept of a kiva as a gathering place embodied the kind of space she wanted to create, and served as the inspiration for Kiva Café's name as well as its design, which she did herself, drawing on her background building adobe homes. (The fact that kivas were often off-limits to women is decidedly *not* subscribed to at Kiva Café!)

"I designed the seating so people would sit with their backs to the wall and, as in the original kivas, have the activity be... directed inward toward the center. The kiva had niches in the wall for the display of artifacts, so I created sixteen niches in the wall for that purpose as well."

The resulting 700-square-foot space might, at first glance, be mistaken for an art gallery. The niches are filled with art—often ceramics— and the walls adorned with large and small paintings and photographs.

Customers sit at four glass-topped tables that double as display cases for jewelry and other handmade objects. Only that customers are sitting, eating, drinking, reading, writing, and talking tells you that Kiva is not a gallery. In addition to all the art on display and for sale, Beebe's own pottery—the mugs and plates used to serve the food and drink—is also for sale.

"The art rotates and is not just for decoration," Beebe explains. "We have openings, which bring the community together and encourage people who have been here to return."

Being across from the entrance to the Holland Tunnel is not picturesque and it discourages foot traffic. But the upside is the vast open space created by the entranceways. Sunlight pours into Kiva's large front window, drenching it with natural light. "We call the front window the TV," says Chris Daly, a rock musician by night and Kiva's manager by day.

Countering the bustling traffic out front is the serene 200-square-foot patio garden out back. It is almost transcendentally peaceful, yet smack-dab in the middle of the city. The combination of quiet plus cityscape—"an urban hideaway" Beebe calls it—reminds her of places in Old World European cities.

Though new construction of residential apartments just north of Kiva and residential conversions within commercial buildings are gradually transforming this part of SoHo, most regular Kiva customers work rather than live nearby. So for now Kiva is not open in the evenings or on weekends (except for special events such as art openings or the "Traveling Palette" dinner series, which features exotic cuisines).

"There are so many different businesses around here," adds Chris. "And although there are many places to buy coffee, people who work in the neighborhood appreciate the quality of Kiva. Many of our customers are two-times-a-day visitors.

They come in the morning between 8 and 10:30 for something quick, often to go, and they return around 2:30. In the morning, they'll buy a large coffee. In the afternoon, a smaller one."

"Coffee is key," says Beebe. "People come in here everyday for coffee and don't even know they could get lunch," adds Chris.

"We had planned to be primarily a coffee place," Beebe continues. "Initially our menu offered much less food than it does now. Just baked goods plus savory tarts, yogurt, granola. But customers started asking for more. Sandwiches, soups, salads, quiche. We added food only because people demanded it. And to generate revenue. Fresh food, simply prepared. Still, coffee—or actually all beverages combined—is forty percent of our income."

For both its brewed coffee and espresso, Kiva Café uses Miscela d'Oro, from Messina, Italy; the Gusto Classico for espresso and FiltrOro for brewed coffee. Decaf is offered only for espresso. "A brewed decaf would just sit in the pot," explains Chris. "With decaf espresso, we can make it fresh."

Loose teas come from SerendipiTea in Long Island City, Queens. Green teas, black teas, and herbal infusions.

Beebe reflects on memorable moments at Kiva: opening day, the blackout when customers sat by candlelight on the street, the Japanese movie crew filming in the café, the old guy on a bike who comes in but never buys a thing, the Traveling Palette Georgian and Uzbekistan dinners.

The conversation ends.

Ten minutes later, Beebe comes running back in. "Oh my god. I almost forgot. I met my husband here!"

Note: A new Kiva Café in Tribeca opened in the spring of 2006 at 139 Reade Street (between Hudson and Greenwich Streets). Subway: 1, 2, 3 to Chambers Street. This location is smaller than the original Kiva—300 square feet with seating for sixteen at four tables plus a counter. Even though it is located only a dozen blocks south of its SoHo counterpart, this new Kiva is in the middle of a residential neighborhood and has a large daytime clientele of freelancers as well as mothers and children. Because of its neighborhood population, it is also open in the evenings and on weekends. And for its many child customers, there are quarter-sized cookies and babycinos: frothed milk, served in an espresso cup!

Short Cups

Given the high SoHo rents, neighborhood cafés are hard-pressed to make a go of it from the sale of coffee primarily. Though not exactly a gathering place, **Joe, the Art of Coffee** at Alessi, the Italian housewares store (130 Greene Street between Houston and Prince), is more a take-out espresso bar (see page 84). Though chains have been assiduously avoided, an exception is made here for **Le Pain Quotidien** (100 Grand Street between Mercer and Greene). And in a pinch, remember the **Angelika Film Center Café** (corner of Houston and Mercer) within the theater. And since SoHo abuts Tribeca (Triangle Below Canal), consider **Little Magazine Café** (161 Hudson Street between Laight and Hubert) and La Colombe Torrefaction (319 Church Street at Lispenard) as well as the Tribeca **Kiva** (139 Reade Street between Greenwich and West Broadway).

· 3 ·

EAST VILLAGE

Bordered by East Houston and 14th Streets and the Bowery and the East River, the East Village has a storied history of welcoming the impoverished, the elderly, the young, and countercultural types of various persuasions. That was before real estate values skyrocketed. Although this has led to a certain homogenization of its population as well as a proliferation of more mainstream businesses, if there are vestiges of the counterculture to be found anywhere in Manhattan, it is most likely here. In addition to Tompkins Square Park, visit the small community gardens, with their sculptures and other wonderful artistic flourishes—before they're replaced by high-rise, high-priced condos.

MudSpot

**307 East 9th Street
(between First and
Second Avenues)
(212) 228-9074
www.themudtruck.com
Open 7AM–midnight
Mon to Fri
8AM–midnight Sat & Sun
Subway: 6 to Astor Place**

MudSpot, an offspring of Mud Truck, the iconic bright orange, gourmet coffee vending truck, is the perfect fit for the East Village. The café—more restaurant on weekends and more coffeehouse during the week—and the neighborhood share a kindred spirit of openness and anti-establishmentism. It would be hard to imagine it located almost anywhere else.

One look at the red and yellow glass tiles that form a peace sign in the sidewalk out front gives

you the first hint of this kinship. Reproductions on MudSpot's website of spider webs spun by household spiders fed caffeine compared with those given marijuana or other mind-altering substances is another hint. So is a quick look on the front of MudSpot's menu: it encourages customers to substitute items! "Please embrace your freedom to substitute, to pick and choose the things you love, everyday, here at the MudSpot."

"It's all about openness," says Greg Northrop, who with his wife Nina Berott, owns MudSpot. "I wanted the experience of coming here to be like the openness and freedom of riding in a convertible."

"If we could have pursued our original vision," adds Nina, "the MudSpot would be a café where you could do whatever you wanted. Ask anything. Say anything. Smoke. Sit with three dogs and a bird on your shoulder. But, we realized we had to comply with certain rules and regulations, so there are limits. Yet, at least esthetically, it did come close to our original vision."

Greg, from Waterbury, Connecticut, and Nina, from Hamburg, Germany, are now committed East Village denizens, living near MudSpot with their two young daughters, Lola Peach and Mimi Free. They met in 1999, when Greg was working as "a glorified office boy" for a PR firm by day and trying to make it as a rock musician. Nina worked for an ad agency. Once Nina became pregnant, their thoughts turned to creating a different lifestyle than that of 9 to 5 office work.

Somehow their "crazy ideas" led them to retrofitting an old Con Ed van to function as a mobile coffee vending truck. "We thought it would be cheaper than renting a place," says Nina.

Seventy thousand dollars in debt, a New York City Mobile Vending Permit in hand, and several cans of orange paint later, the MudTruck—the city's first mobile vendor of gourmet coffee and espresso drinks—was ready for business. "Mud" was what Greg's Italian grandmother had called her strong, thick coffee. Orange, because Nina felt there was no orange on the streets of New York. "Yellow taxis. Yellow school buses. Brown UPS trucks. Red fire trucks. White and blue police cars and buses. And, of course, green Starbucks. But no orange."

That was in March 2001. Two and a half years later, MudSpot opened. "The MudTruck was too risky a business by itself," says Greg. "Anything could happen. The truck could break down on route. There could be an accident. Or a problem with equipment. Or some cop who feels like hassling us and demanding we move, even though we have a permit. Renting a place minimized some of those risks. And, beyond that, opening up a café allowed us to spread our energy. Spread the radiance and warmth of orange. Hold out our hands to the sun. Let it shine."

Located on a block of small, independently-owned businesses (including a witch-craft/occult supply store and more women's clothing boutiques than one can count), this block of Ninth Street is rich in East Village music and counterculture history.

MudSpot itself is located in what was once the street-level apartment of an East Village character, Perry Gerwitz, who often played a stand-in for Woody Allen. A framed picture of Perry with other cast members (including Donald Sutherland) from one of his movies hangs on the wall. And in the basement Adam Horovitz supposedly recorded a vinyl record before he became a Beastie Boy—The Young and Useless recording of *Real Men Don't Floss*, released on Ratcage Records.

Jimi Hendrix is said to have lived in the basement a few doors down, at 321 Ninth Street. Further down the block, the Doors' Jim Morrison lived with his wife, Patricia Kennealy Morrison, who continues to live there. She once had a bone to pick with MudSpot for bricking over the name "Eowyn" (a character in the The Lord of the Rings), which had been inscribed in the concrete out front. "It created a kind of rise on which someone could trip," says Nina in their defense. "We gave Patricia photos of the name... she thanked us for doing that."

Although some might be quick to say MudSpot has an old hippie look and feel to it, it is much softer and less raw than the 1960s East Village hippie style at its apex. Yes, there is an American flag with the stars reconfigured to create a peace sign, but that is about as demonstrative as it gets.

Inside this slender storefront, the front area with its counter and stools is so narrow that two people cannot pass through at the same time. This is also the noisiest and busiest part of the café. Past this, the café opens up—with, maybe, eight tables—into a darker, quieter space. And blessedly, an outdoor garden covered by a glass roof and filled with long tables for communal seating is bright, cozy, and quiet. It is where those who come to spend long quiet time head for writing, reading, or intimate conversation. "It is great when the sun hits it directly," Greg says. "And when it snows, it is beautiful."

For music aficionados, there is a constant stream of carefully chosen selections. Someone other than Cat Stevens singing a Cat Stevens song, for instance. The reggae classic, "The Harder They Fall," but not by Jimmy Cliff. That kind of esoterica.

"Music is the specialty of the house," says Nina. "It is as important to our coffee operation as milk and sugar. We leave lots of freedom to our Mudtenders, but the music should always be something that leaves a positive 'orange' feeling."

"Lively tunes in the morning, calmer songs at lunch, and rock 'n' roll after dark," Greg adds.

Since it all began with the MudTruck, coffee continues to reign supreme at MudSpot, despite an extensive menu of breakfast dishes as well as panini, burritos, quesadillas, salads, and soups for later in the day. In homage to MudSpot's coffee origins is the "Mud Burrito," made with *espresso-glazed* rice and beans.

The house brew is the original MudTruck Blend, from Porto Rico Importing Co. on nearby St. Mark's Place. Greg, who had no background in coffee ("I'm a beer drinker!"), spent eight or nine months testing before settling on this blend, which he calls "an extremely complex, naturally sweet, highly caffeinated blend with low acidity and no bitterness." Not bad for a beer drinker.

The resulting strong, thick brew would make Greg's grandmother, the original mud maker, proud. Many agree. The *Onion* satirical newspaper, the *Village Voice*, *Time Out New York*, the *New York Times*, and others have all sung its praises. "We've been able to turn a negative—that is, 'mud,'—into a positive," say Greg and Nina almost in unison.

For espresso drinks, MudSpot uses their Mojo Blend, a "roasty," dark Italian-style coffee. Served in glass tumblers and pulled as two shot espressos on an Italian-made Wega two-group espresso machine, the taste is spicy but smooth, with lots of crema.

MudSpot also sells coffee by the pound in the café or online. Greg recommends their Hippie Blend: "Green-friendly, bird-friendly, rainforest-friendly, you name it," says Greg. "You could call it our 'Greenrainbird' blend."

During weekday mornings and afternoons, regular customers—about 90 percent of whom Greg and Nina say are local residents—settle in with coffee plus. Mud regulars form a tight community who are intensely loyal and proud to patronize this unabashedly anti-Starbucks alternative in a neighborhood where Starbucks branches abound.

As at most cafés, the daytime crowd is mostly young ("I'm no longer in our target audience," bemoans the forty-something Greg), but anyone can, and does, feel comfortable here. MudSpot is, after all, about openness.

"People are proud to get their coffee from MudSpot," says Greg. "The feeling is, 'This is my spot. My café...' What I hope for when they come here is that they walk out of New York. That it be like stepping into the country. The buzz goes away. The street noise goes away. There is no attitude. No aggression."

Note: In addition to the MudSpot, the Mud coffee chain includes the MudTruck at Astor Place (in front of the subway station), Union Square (14th Street and Broadway), Wall Street (near the New York Stock Exchange), and Sheridan Square. And there is a Mud Coffee Bar at

Kiehl's, the skin care products apothecary at 109 Third Avenue (at 13th Street). The MudTruck at Astor Place is there consistently from 7AM to 6PM every day. The hours at the other locations are less regular.

The bright orange MudTrucks (each fitted with three sinks, an espresso machine, refrigerator, grinder, and storage space) are a well-known and warmly embraced part of the New York City streetscape. When the original MudTruck opened in 2001 at Astor Place, sandwiched between two of the city's largest Starbucks, it quickly gained a loyal clientele, most of whom saw the act of buying coffee there as a vote for the little guy as well as a vote against Starbucks hegemony.

"At first it was day to day," recalls Nina. "A few curious people showed up the first day. And the next day those curious people brought some of their curious friends, who then brought some of their friends, and so on. Soon we had hundreds of customers. It really was something out of Malcolm Gladwell's *Tipping Point*. And, I have to say, we got all this incredible press. It was as if they had nothing else to write about. No news. We became the morning segment on TV talk shows."

The newest expansion to the business is the use of MudTrucks for catering film shoots in the evening. The MudTrucks have provided film crews with coffee on the sets of such movies as *Eternal Sunshine of the Spotless Mind* (which coincided with Jim Carrey's birthday) and *The Devil Wears Prada*. "On the set of the movie *American Gangster*," Nina and Greg reminisce, "we almost ran over Russell Crowe. As we were leaving, he ran out in front of the truck to tell us that we'd made a lot of people very happy—and almost got hit in the process."

Look out for more orange trucks!

Ninth Street Espresso

**700 East 9th Street
(at corner of Avenue C)
(212) 358-9225
www.ninthstrectespresso.com
Open 7AM–7PM daily
Subway: L to First Avenue**

Ninth Street Espresso is a little espresso bar with a big reputation. Why else would all the cars with out-of-state plates be lined up out front on any given weekend?

For one of the best espressos to be had anywhere. The *Village Voice* voted it best espresso outside of Seattle. *Food & Wine* magazine called it among the best in the entire country. Which explains why out-of-town coffee aficionados find their way to this far, far East Village outpost, in Alphabet City, where the avenues become lettered.

There is no hype behind this reputation. The renown won by this unadorned coffee shop, with its ten tables, one small stand-up counter, and stripped down menu is well-earned and well-secured. In the words of one serious coffee blogger, who refers to Ninth Street Espresso as an "Alphabet City Mecca": "It is the quintessential neighborhood joint with a global reputation. Great coffee, done right, zero bullshit."

Ken Nye, Ninth Street Espresso's founder and guiding spirit, was preparing to be a force in the artisanal coffee movement for most of his life. He just didn't know it. He was well into adulthood when he realized that his fascination with coffee and café culture began when he was a young boy.

"We lived on the Upper West Side of Manhattan—110th Street between Broadway and Amsterdam—and my father loved going to the Hungarian Pastry Shop (see page 130). To me, a seven-year-old kid, the place just had this incredible mystique. Always crowded and all these very intense conversations going on. And I remember the smell of the coffee. I loved it."

When he reached drinking age—that is, *coffee* drinking age—in his late teens, he drank the same bad deli coffee out of blue Greek diner paper cups as everyone else in New York. He didn't know any better. At about 21, he encountered his first coffee roaster. The guy who operated the machine touted the joys of fresh roasted coffee. Once again, he fell in love with the smells.

His curiosity and interest in coffee and the different ways of preparing it continued to grow, though by now he owned a bar in the East Village, so his daytime preoccupation was with alcohol.

Then his future brother-in-law began sending him fresh roasted coffees from the West Coast. And according to Ken, "That was it. I was hooked. I never looked back... I learned everything I possibly could about coffee and its preparation. I became obsessed, to the annoyance of my wife.

"By the year 2000, I decided to take the risk. To see if New York City was ready to accept an artisanal coffee bar [Ninth Street Espresso is considered the city's first], which I could combine with a community coffeehouse. I wanted both. Good coffee and a café. I liked the idea that drinking coffee was part of a ritual.

"I chose the East Village because I worked in the East Village and lived there [in Ninth Street Espresso's building]... I liked the energy and felt the neighborhood could benefit from a café. The East Village is really special... Although there's been gentrification, it is still considered a fringe neighborhood—and I say that with love. There is a Latino culture here. An Afro-American one. And all these students—from NYU, Cooper [Cooper Union], and SVA [School of Visual Arts]. There is a rough-edged, non-conformist culture that is still a magnet for progressive, strong-willed young people.

"The park across the street is what made me take this space and not others," he confesses. "I would have established the business faster on the avenue, but here I'm across the street from this gorgeous community garden with that incredible willow tree. When it's in full bloom, you can't even see the houses on the other side of the park. And we get to watch that cool hawk that lives in the park. We get to watch it hunt."

From its inception at the end of 2000, there was never any chance that Ninth Street Espresso was going to be a typical café. It was to be totally espresso driven. Following the Northern Italian example, brewed coffee is not even offered. And while tea and chai are on the menu, maybe two customers out of a hundred order it. (It's like going to Peter Luger's Steakhouse and ordering the cod: Why bother?)

Ken has never considered having any substantial food. Pastries come from the highly regarded Balthazar, but when the offerings—croissants, pain au chocolat, oat scones, sticky buns, orange brioche—run out, usually around 1PM, they are not replenished.

"I keep streamlining things. Cutting back. We offer less and less as time goes on. This allows us to focus on the espresso," says Ken, "and at the same time allows us to offer it in an environment you can enjoy." A full thirty percent of the café's total space is given over to a work area for making espresso efficiently and fast.

"We are not profit driven. We are product driven. If people want to call us snobs or think we take coffee too seriously, that's okay. But the bottom line is we're an espresso driven business—seventy percent of our revenue comes from pulling espresso shots—and that's ahead of being a really cool café. We want to be at the forefront of the espresso movement. We're humble about that. We're learning about it everyday."

Ninth Street's coffee roaster is Counter Culture Coffee of Durham, North Carolina, an environmentally conscious company that was among the first to make organic, all shade-grown coffees available. Ninth Street uses their Espresso Toscano blend, which is a Brazil-based coffee combined with two very contrasting Sumatra beans, roasted in the Northern Italian tradition. The result is a sweet and mild espresso with hints of caramel, hazelnut, and dark chocolate.

In addition, each day Ninth Street highlights what they call a micro-lot coffee from a single farm. These coffees are made by the French press method (in a plunger pot, water is forced over and through coarsely ground beans, and then left to sit for two to four minutes).

For the first several years, Ninth Street used a Faema E61 Legend (the world's first pump-operated espresso machine, created in 1961), but around 2006, it switched to a two-group Synesso Cyncra, a handcrafted espresso machine manufactured in Seattle. "We got incredible results on the original Faema. But it required lots of work," Ken says. "We are purists only to a point. It was okay to let go of it and get a modern machine."

By the time you read this, the two-group Synesso, which Ken Nye claims must be the most heavily trafficked two-group machine in the country, will have been replaced by a three-group.

The baristas at Ninth Street Espresso—mostly heavily tattooed young men—are primarily from the West Coast and are all incredibly skilled. "They are highly accomplished artists, musicians, dancers who choose to be baristas because… they love espresso in a foodie kind of way, and it's fun to work here. Great staff. Great customers. And I pay them better than any other baristas in the country," Ken adds. "Which doesn't mean they're getting rich."

"We regularly have espresso workshops for staff," he continues. "We do cuppings every week to develop palates. You can't advance as a barista without a developed palate. And we're totally transparent, meaning we exchange information with roasters and other baristas all the time. We don't believe in being secretive. Apparently there are some espresso bars in Italy where they actually put shrouds over the espresso machine so no one can see how the barista works. We go in the other direction… We want to see the standard for making espresso elevated nationwide."

One signpost of having achieved a high standard is the latte art that graces all the frothed milk espresso drinks at Ninth Street, something all its baristas can do with aplomb. Some do it more ornately than others, perhaps, but every drink with froth milk has it. And black and white photos of latte art grace the walls.

"It's not a sales gimmick," Ken is quick to say. "It's the signature of a skilled barista. It tells me the barista is in absolute control of his craft. You can only do latte art if you get the texture of the milk right and you pour it correctly. Once a barista gets really good at texturing and pouring, it's hard not to do latte art!"

Although weekends may bring out-of-towners to Ninth Street Espresso, the weekday business is a local affair. Asked to describe the demographic of his customers, Ken says it is impossible to do. "Someone once suggested that if Noah's Ark was filled with people rather than animals, it would look like Ninth Street Espresso.

"On a warm day, they'll be 20 people inside and another 40 or 50 congregating out front. The energy here is alive and electric. People who might not be tolerant of each other in the outside world are incredibly tolerant here at the café. A right-wing cop from next door can come in and there is no tension. No grief. No ill-will. Sometimes the banter gets loud and out of hand. It can get serious, but it's never threatening… My idea of what a café should be is a place with no boundaries. I should be able to be anyone I want to be here and be that person with absolute comfort. Be whomever I want to be. Say whatever is on my mind.

"Although I once did ask a mother of a toddler, who was naked and rolling around on the floor among the customers, to pick up her daughter. The mother became indignant. Told me the baby was only expressing herself, and that I was trying to stifle that. We're that kind of place."

House Rules, such as they are, are posted on the wall:

—No cell phones at the counter
—No "half decaf/half regular"
—No pets in the café
—No dogs blocking the door

—Cash only

—Restroom for customers only

—Be nice or go home

And, at the very bottom as a kind of addendum:

Unattended children will be given an espresso and a free dog.

A coffee roaster's website said that although Ninth Street was typically, and justly, praised for its coffee, it delivers "the whole package": it has great coffee, and is also a great café with great energy. The same energy that Ken Nye encountered on his boyhood visits with his father to the Hungarian Pastry Shop so many years ago.

Note: In January of 2007, Ninth Street Espresso opened a café inside the Classic Stage Company theater, at 136 East 13th Street (between Third and Fourth Avenues). Subway: L to Third Avenue. It has since been sold to one of Ninth Street's baristas, and is now called **Everyman Espresso**.

As for opening other branches, Ken Nye worries that they would not be able to capture the same energy as the far East Village location. This fear, plus the reality of the New York real estate market, makes him less than sanguine about the future of artisanal coffee in Manhattan. With rents from $100 to $200 a square foot, it becomes hard, if not impossible, to survive as a coffee oriented café. "Cafés in the Pacific Northwest," he says, "don't want to expand into New York City. Why pay New York City rents, when for that money you can buy three buildings in Seattle?"

Despite these misgivings, a recent decision was made to open another location in the Chelsea Market (75 Ninth Avenue between 15th and 16th Streets). Subway: A, C, E to 14th Street. Joining about twenty other specialty shops in the old National Biscuit Company building, and with thousands of visitors a day, it is anticipated that this will be Ninth Street's flagship location. A case of Ninth *Street* Espresso morphing into Ninth *Avenue* Espresso?

Short Cups

The East Village abounds with cafés, thanks to rents somewhat less than other Manhattan neighborhoods and to a residential population of young hipsters, students, and freelancers, a prime demographic for those who indulge in café life. Some worthy places include: **Café Pick Me Up** (145 Avenue A at 9th Street); **Chez Betty** (256 East 3rd Street at Avenue C); **Cuppa Cuppa** (75 East 4th Street between Bowery and Second Avenue); **Rapture Café & Books** (200 Avenue A between 12th and 13th); **17 Bleecker** (17 Bleecker Street near Elizabeth); and **Tarallucci e Vino** (163 First Avenue at 10th Street). As a sign of the times, the quintessential East Village café, **Alt.Cafe**, which opened in 1995, recently closed to reopen as **Hopscotch**. Its owner cited changes in the neighborhood, most obviously rising rents, insurance, and other costs and a burgeoning population of parents with young kids—the "stroller crowd"—to which the café in its new incarnation will cater.

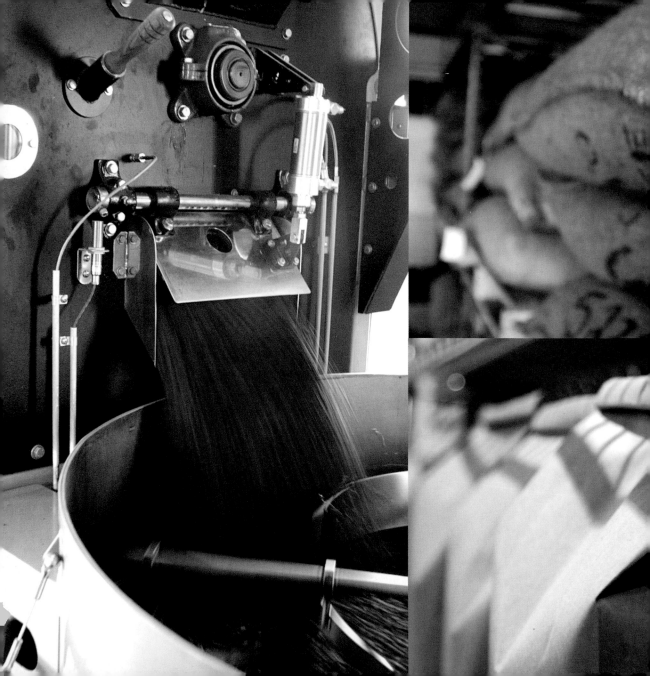

· 4 ·

WEST VILLAGE

Alternatively referred to as Greenwich Village or simply the Village, the West Village lies west of Broadway and east of the Hudson River, between 14th Street to the north and Houston Street to the south. A diverse neighborhood, the Village is different things to different people. A college campus (NYU seemingly owns half the real estate). A tourist destination. A place to visit for dining, music, art, theater, and film. A busy commercial district along the avenues. Meandering, serene residential blocks between the river and Hudson Street. Objectively no longer the bohemian, artist quarter it once was, that legacy and spirit nevertheless lingers.

Grounded

Organic Coffee & Tea House
28 Jane Street
(between West 4th & Greenwich Avenue)
(212) 647-0943
www.basictea.com
(for online loose tea purchasing)
Open 7AM–8PM Mon to Fri
7:30AM–8PM Sat & Sun
Subway: A, C, E to 14th Street

Grounded Organic Coffee & Tea House is the kind of neighborhood place that local residents jealously guard as their own. Located in the part of the Village where the city's reliable street grid goes haywire and somehow West 4th Street comes out above West 10th, it is not likely that even New Yorkers will stumble upon it. Jen Greenberg, who with her brother Mark owns Grounded, says "I know people who live maybe five blocks away who say, 'I didn't even know you were here.' And we've been here for two years!"

Occupying a nearly 100-year-old building that was in earlier incarnations a carriage house, a printing house, and an antique furniture business, Grounded sits in the middle of a quiet block that would have warmed the heart of Jane Jacobs, the social critic and urbanist who sang the praises of such mixed-use blocks. She lived for many years a few blocks away on Hudson Street.

With a bronze fixture factory across the street, restaurants on both corners, a parking garage, high-rise and low-rise apartment buildings, a few elegant townhouses and some other establishments of indeterminate origin and use, this particular block of Jane Street epitomizes mixed-use in the best sense of the word. With relatively little traffic, it is the quiet kind of block that cries out for sitting on stoops—if only there were more stoops.

It is the perfect block for this easygoing gathering place. In Jen's words, "an old school Greenwich Village coffeehouse." Or, as Mark puts it, "a downscale place in what has become an insanely upscale neighborhood."

Jen and Mark, who are both in their thirties, got from their native Cincinnati to Greenwich Village via different routes. Jen left Cincinnati to work in the restaurant world as both a bartender and waitress, including a stint in the Virgin Islands. Mark established a reggae music store and a gift shop in Cincinnati. Jen was the first to settle in the Village, which had always held an allure for her. (She now has only a ten-minute walk to work. "I love that!" she says.) When Mark's wife was offered a teaching position nearby, he too found himself in the New York area.

Both were looking for something new—something they could do together. Jen liked the food and beverage service business, and Mark had always had an interest in coffee and enjoyed hanging out in coffeehouses. "No, really," he says, somewhat defensively. "The Midwest has a surprisingly good café culture. In the neighborhood of the University of Cincinnati there are some very good coffeehouses… Nice homey atmosphere. It's New York that was behind and needed to catch up."

The former carriage house with its giant skylight—"the early morning light that comes through at 7:30AM while classical music is playing on WQXR creates great ambiance," claims Mark—made the decision for them. It was the perfect space on the perfect block in the perfect neighborhood for the kind of coffeehouse they envisioned.

A quick, mostly-do-it-yourself, no-frills renovation resulted in a surprisingly comfortable and pleasant space: about twenty small tables, a counter and stools along one wall, a bookcase filled with donated books for a lending library, a soft and comfy red sofa against the far wall (a favored destination for mothers), and plants galore, even a small lemon tree that grows directly below the skylight.

Photographs by family or friends grace the walls, changing periodically, and on a shelf opposite the front prep area are blue espresso cups, which were supposedly used by C.S. Lewis, author of *The Chronicles of Narnia*. And in the rear, the big old-fashioned lamp with antique shade, fondly referred to as the "Grand Dame."

The comfort of Grounded is almost paradoxical, given the painted concrete floors and brick walls, the exposed pipes, radiators, and other plumbing and electrical appurtenances. The space radiates warmth despite cold concrete, and looks finished despite exposed pipes and wires. Maybe the skylight works the magic.

"Perhaps if we had lots of money," says Mark, "we would have tried to zing the place up. But we didn't, so we didn't." Grounded is as down-to-earth as its name implies.

"It was slow at the beginning," Mark says, "and I was a little worried about us

making it… But I came in one Sunday morning, about two months after we opened, and saw a long line of customers. At that moment, I realized we would be successful."

Like most gathering places that depend on people not working a 9 to 5 job, Grounded attracts a youngish crowd—students, actors and actresses, freelance writers, stay-at-home-moms. There is always a smattering of older customers, but still the customer profile skews toward the young and toward the computer crowd.

The Greenbergs acknowledge the heavy use of laptops throughout the day—less so in the evenings—encouraged by the availability of free wireless access. About the computer use, Jen says, "It is a big part of the place. I admit that it can take away from the community vibe… but after work, there is much more talking and fewer computers."

Ensconced unobtrusively in a quiet neighborhood, it is not surprising that a huge part of Grounded's business is comprised of regulars. Less so on weekends, with tourists and visitors wandering around the Village, especially on nearby Bleecker Street, which Jen calls the Village's "Rodeo Drive."

Although Grounded's owners take their coffee and tea seriously, they consider themselves "purists" more in the sense of their devotion to organic products. This commitment to things organic includes not only the coffee and tea, but the milk, baked goods, and most of the soups, salads, sandwiches, and panini they offer.

Mark, who has been a vegetarian for nearly twenty years and has always taken organic, sustainable farming seriously, believes Grounded might be one of the only cafés in New York City that uses organic milk. "The organic milk costs us double the price, but our customers don't know that. Our coffee prices are still standard. And we don't charge extra for soy milk even. Why should a person be punished for their lactose intolerance?"

The people who initially trained Jen and staff were from one of Grounded's major coffee suppliers, Portland Roasting Company, an Oregon, environmentally conscious micro-roaster of organically grown—often shade grown—"Farm Friendly" specialty coffees. Portland's Organic Teramo blend—a combination of Indonesian, Central American, and African coffees, medium-dark roasted—gives Grounded's espresso its slight berry finish.

The house brewed coffee—Moka Sumatra, a combination of Nicaraguan and Sumatran coffees—comes from Dean's Beans of Orange, Massachusetts, another progressive coffee roaster committed to organic and Fair Trade coffees. Dean's goes one step further than other such roasters, providing coffee beans that are not only organically grown but kosher as well!

Jen characterizes their espresso making as a "mix" of purist and fearless: "I am not scared to add chocolate or caramel." The availability of such drinks as "Café BonBon" (double shot of espresso plus a layer of condensed milk), "Sweet-N-Nutty" (latte with hazelnut and caramel), "Café Aloha" (espresso with steamed coconut and regular milk) or "Mint Kiss Latte" (espresso, chocolate, and mint) underscores that lack of fear. Although Grounded sells less tea than coffee, it in no way plays second fiddle.

The same attention to source and preparation given to coffee is also spent on tea. They offer nineteen different loose teas, all available by cup or pot (or on their website at www.basictea.com): black, green, herbal, oolong, white (from the leaves picked before they've gone through the oxidation process, resulting in a mild tea with somewhat less caffeine than green tea), as well as some blends. And rooibos, a "red tea" from South Africa that is really not a tea. "It tastes a little smoky," says Jen. "A kind of earthy smoky. Reminds me of my Dad's pipe tobacco."

Just as staff are trained in the particulars for making excellent coffee, so too with making tea. "All tea leaves come from the same plant. They're just picked at different times and dried differently. Which means they have to be prepared differently. For example," Jen continues, "we don't use boiling water for the green, white, and oolong teas. It would over-extract them and make them bitter. Instead, the water should be 190 degrees. Black teas, however, do require boiling water. And, of course, the steeping times and the amount of tea used differ for each kind of tea."

If it is the caffeine that one craves, tea can satisfy that need as well as coffee. "Some days," says Jen, "I'll just drink several pots of green tea over the course of the day. It gives me my caffeine fix. Just a slower injection!"

Coffee, tea, or milk—organic all—Grounded is doing the right thing in the right place. The Greenberg siblings talk with great pride of various European tourists who chanced upon Grounded at the beginning of their New York visits, and returned every day they remained. "That," says Jen Greenberg, "proves we're doing it right!"

Joe, the Art of Coffee

**141 Waverly Place
(between Sixth Avenue & Gay Street)
(212) 924-6750
www.joetheartofcoffee.com
Open 7AM–8PM Mon to Fri
8AM–8PM Sat & Sun
Subway: A, B, C, D, E, F, V to West 4th St**

The buzz about Joe is not just from the caffeine. From almost the first moment this West Village café opened its doors in the summer of 2003, it has been called one of the city's best places to get a cup of West Coast/Seattle-style coffee. *Time Out New York* gave it its "Eat Out Award" for best coffee in New York in 2004, and in 2006, Joe was voted that magazine's Readers' Choice for "Best Nonchain Coffee Purveyor."

This is exactly what its founder, Jonathan Rubinstein, set out to do. "I knew I wanted to start a nice looking, community based place," he admits, "but the emphasis was always going to be the coffee."

To this day, he eschews serving soups, salads, and sandwiches. "Then the focus would no longer be the coffee," he says. "If I ever started serving those things, I'd soon go out of business." He does, however, sell pastry, culled from about eight of the city's best bakeries.

Jonathan Rubinstein's path to coffee purveyor par excellence was not a straight one. He worked as a talent agent representing television and movie actors for a number of years, and only after he quit did he begin to think about what else he might do with his life. In his early thirties at the time, he had a vague notion of wanting to do something completely different. "Something fun, exciting, and romantic—and maybe even useful."

After dismissing the possibility of starting a summer camp on Long Island or his own management company, he came to the coffeehouse idea. His family had always loved coffee. He remembered coming to New York City on family vacations, and spending half their time looking for a good cup of coffee. At the time, New York lacked places that raised coffee to the level of culinary art as it was in Seattle, Portland, and San Francisco.

Although New York had long been regarded a food mecca, coffee aficionados found its coffee the worst of any major city in the world. "It was crazy. We would spend $30 a day trying to find good coffee," he remembers. "There was just this tremendous void."

He found a former dry cleaners on Waverly Place that had long been empty, deemed too small and on too quiet a residential block to have sufficient street traffic to support most commercial enterprises. But it seemed the perfect location for the kind of intimate, neighborhood café that Jonathan had in mind, and the rent was relatively cheap.

"I then spent five months scrambling around, trying to learn everything there was to know about coffee… I was going to find the greatest roasters, and… put that money in the budget, even if that was going to be our biggest cost. Using the best coffee available was going to be an absolute."

Around that time, his sister Gabrielle, an opera singer who had spent a summer at Tanglewood, in Lenox, Massachusetts, told him that she'd found a coffeehouse with the greatest coffee she'd ever had. But she couldn't remember its name!

"Shortly afterwards," Jonathan recalls, "I met some friends at a dinner party who mentioned a phenomenal coffeehouse in the Berkshires, and it turned out to be the same place"—the Barrington Coffee Roasting Company of Great Barrington, Massachusetts, a company started by folks who first began roasting coffee beans in a hot air popper in their college dorm. They wanted to get into the New York market and mentor someone as passionate about coffee as they are. Barrington Coffee Roasters and Joe's was the perfect match.

A crash course given by Barrington Roasters in everything one needed to know about coffee followed: how to pull a perfect ounce-and-a-quarter, straight ristretto shot of espresso; how to make the perfect foam needed for lattes, cappuccinos, and macchiatos; and how to create latte art. They provided the coffee, a Vienna roasted Panamanian bean, the lightest of the darkest roasts, and even sent Jonathan one of his first baristas, Amanda Byron, who moved to New York City to pursue an acting career. Her day job remains co-director of coffee at Joe's. (Erin Meister is the other co-director.)

Jonathan purchased a top-of-the-line La Marzocco espresso machine, setting him back the equivalent of a new Japanese compact automobile. That machine has since been replaced by a Synesso Cyncra, custom-built by a former La Marzocco engineer—one of the first hundred such machines sold.

It did not take long before validation came, in the form of the pastry chef from nearby Babbo's restaurant (of Mario Batali fame) who, not long after Joe's had been open, sauntered in and announced, "I have never had coffee like this outside of Italy!"

"That was my first rock star experience," Jonathan sheepishly admits. Chefs and other customers have continued to sing his coffee's praises. And, if there was ever any doubt, the crowds in front of Joe's, on an otherwise sleepy, almost somnolent, non-commercial stretch (the worst location possible, he was warned), book-ended by two Starbucks, each a block away ("Doesn't bother me in the slightest") tell him he is doing something right.

About a dozen small, bright yellow tables (think lemon tart) grace this surprisingly bright and airy space. The sometimes very long take-out line, up the middle of the café and even out the door, might make for an uncomfortable, crowded feeling, but the atmosphere is welcoming, and customers—an inordinately large number of whom are regulars—often settle into their seats for long stays. That his is a neighborhood gathering place pleases Jonathan. "I wanted to avoid the Seattle mindset—the arrogance that conveys the feeling that we're doing you a favor by giving you a great cup of coffee."

Due to its West Village location, there was initially some concern that Joe's would become known as a celebrity coffee bar. (Joe does, incidentally, provide the coffee for the Letterman show.) Indeed, many celebrities live in this hip and historical neighborhood and do quite naturally patronize the café. The actor/director Philip Seymour Hoffman has been a regular customer, as have other actors and actresses: Daniel Day-Lewis, Sam Shepard, Jessica Lange, Jake and Maggie Gyllenhaal (though she has moved to Park Slope), Janeane Garofalo, and Matthew Modine. The *New Yorker* magazine writer Malcolm Gladwell (author of *Blink* and *The Tipping Point*) comes by, as does comedienne Amy Sedaris, who has been known to come in with a tray of home-baked cupcakes, in exchange for cash.

The clientele at Joe's is a reflection of the neighborhood. Yes, some celebrities, but mostly just a cross-section of typical Village denizens: actors, writers, artists, musicians, graphic designers, computer programmers, and freelancers of every kind—who else is able to while away a couple of hours over a latte in the middle of the week, in the middle of the day?

The passion about coffee that served as the impetus for starting Joe's has not waned one bit. Jonathan's original five-year plan was to start five cafés, and now he has three. His next place, he hopes, will be larger, allowing him to sell his superlative espresso in a comfortable setting, accommodate more people, and give him room to sell coffee-related items such as brewing equipment, beans, cups and saucers, and even books. And he'd like to give more classes about coffee, an expansion of the infrequent (maybe once a month) "Coffee 101" class he now offers.

"I love it," he practically intones. "I love it now more than at the beginning… Maybe it sounds a little cheesy, but a great cup of coffee is like a little cup of sunshine to start the day. A way to spread a little happiness. A little joy."

Cheesy? Maybe. True nonetheless.

Note: There are now two additional Joe locations. Joe, the Art of Coffee at 9 East 13th Street (between Fifth Avenue and University Place) opened in March 2005. Subway: 4, 5, 6, L, N, Q, R, W to 14th St./Union Sq. Station. This Joe branch has a very different feel from the Waverly Place location. Because of its proximity to the New School, its customer base during the week is mostly students, faculty, and staff. It doesn't have, "the strange West Village energy that the Waverly place does," Jonathan says. "It's more like a Starbucks… more iPods and computers."

And, he explains, it has a completely different rhythm. Whereas 13th Street's busiest day is Monday ("because students are not happy to go back to class, and need the extra boost coffee gives them"), the absolute slowest day at Waverly place is Monday. "People make the resolution over the weekend to start making their own coffee in the morning. So, Monday is slow. By Tuesday, they've already broken their resolution, and business is back to normal." And whereas 13th Street is busiest during the week (classes in session), Waverly Place is busiest on weekends, the only time it can realistically be a destination for those who live and work elsewhere.

In the summer of 2006, Jonathan was asked to set up the coffee bar in the new Alessi home goods store in Soho: Joe at Alessi, 130 Greene Street (at Prince Street). Subway: B, D, F, V to Broadway–Lafayette; N, R to Prince Street. This one is very much an Italian espresso bar with limited seating. "It has a good positive energy," Jonathan says, "but it's primarily a stand-up, run-in, run-out café, typical of those one finds all over Italy."

Look for more Joes in the future—remember the five-year, five-place plan— although Jonathan swears, that no matter how many cafés he might open, Waverly Place will always be the flagship. "It's the most meaningful," he says somewhat wistfully.

Short Cups

Greenwich Village café culture is well established and venerable, although the coffeehouses made famous during the Beat Generation have long since closed. Some of the old Italian coffeehouses remain, but they are now largely tourist destinations. Among the many contemporary cafés deserving of mention are: **Brewbar** (327 West 11th Street between Washington and Greenwich), which is owned by the nearby Abington Guest House; **Doma Café and Gallery** (17 Perry Street at Waverly); **Esperanto Café** (114 MacDougal Street between 3rd and Bleecker); **Jack's Stir Brew** (138 West 10th Street between Greenwich and Waverly); **Mojo Coffee** (128 Perry Street between Greenwich and Washington); **The Point** (37a Bedford Street between Carmine and Downing), inside a yarn store—hence its name; **'Snice** (45 Eighth Avenue at West 4th); **Tea Spot** (127 Sullivan Street at West 3rd); and **Think** (248 Mercer Street between 3rd and 4th). In the summer of 2007, **Irving Farm Coffee Company** (56 Seventh Avenue between 13th and 14th) opened (see page 95).

· 5 ·

GRAMERCY / UNION SQUARE

The adjoining neighborhoods of Gramercy and Union Square together comprise the area east of Fifth Avenue to First Avenue, between 14th Street and about 23rd Street. Both are defined by their parks, which are as different as the neighborhoods themselves. Gramercy Park is as exclusive (only certain townhouse residents around the park have keys to it) as Union Square Park is inclusive (its year-round farmer's market, for example, is a magnet for people from all over). Gramercy is a rather rarefied, absolutely quaint and elegant, mostly residential enclave, while Union Square is an inimitable New York City amalgam of commercial, residential, and entertainment activity. Busy by day and busy by night. By comparison, at night, Gramercy sleeps.

71 Irving Place: Coffee & Tea Bar

71 Irving Place
(between 18th & 19th Streets)
(212) 995-5252
www.irvingfarm.com
Open 7AM–11PM Mon to Wed
7AM–midnight Thurs & Fri
8AM–midnight Sat; 8AM–11PM Sun
Subway: L, N, Q, R, W, 4, 5, 6 to 14th St/
Union Square; 6 to 23rd Street

Many cafés emphasize either their coffee or their atmosphere. 71 Irving Place gives equal importance to both. This instantly appealing café, the ground floor of a 19th-century Greek Revival townhouse, is a much loved neighborhood gathering place.

Not only is the coffee very good ("Best Cup of Coffee" in New York City, according to *New York* magazine)—it is its very own! Since 1999, after the purchase and renovation of what had once been a working farm in upstate Millerton, New York, Irving Farms has supplied the beans to 71 Irving as well as to other cafés, restaurants, and food stores within and without the New York metropolitan area (Whole Foods, Dean & Deluca, Gourmet Garage, City Bakery, and Petrossian, to name some).

"That we roast our own coffee sets us apart from other cafés," says Steve Leven, one of the owners of the café and the roasting company. "We know coffee. We study it, and it comes through as part of the culture in the café."

Steve Leven, who grew up in Maryland and moved to New York to study film at NYU, started the café with his business partner, David Elwell, in 1996. "While going to film school at NYU, I hung out in cafés around the city. Then I lived in this neighborhood for a number of years, and although there was a diner and there were bars, there was nothing like a coffeehouse that could bring the neighborhood together. That's what I wanted to do," he says.

Leven describes 71 Irving as having been "a shell" when they took it over. Renovations included new wainscoting, a new floor, and an old bar. Leven calls the

bar "my favorite object in the place… discovered in a Harlem warehouse and said to have been the oldest bar in Williamsburg, Brooklyn." And the space came with an unusual architectural feature: a set of stairs to nowhere. A Hollywood writer, George Axelrod (*The Manchurian Candidate*, *Breakfast at Tiffany's*), lived here, and he made use of this odd staircase in his screenplay for Billy Wilder's *Seven Year Itch*:

Marilyn Monroe: This is a nicer apartment than the Kaufmans'. For instance, the Kaufmans have no stairs. Hey, where do they lead to?
Tom Ewell: No place.
Marilyn Monroe: No place? A stairway to nowhere. That's elegant.
Tom Ewell: I wouldn't say elegant. You see, this used to be a duplex. The landlord made two apartments out of it by boarding up your floor.
Marilyn Monroe: Oh, yes, I remember that patch in the floor. I dropped my cuticle pusher down the crack. Cuticle pusher. Yeah.

Today big burlap bags of coffee beans are stored on the stairs.

Norman Thomas, the Socialist Party candidate for president in every election (six!) between 1928 and 1948, also lived at 71 Irving, and his wife Violet had a tearoom in the building in the 1930s and 1940s.

Not long after opening the original café, Steve and David decided they wanted to create a brand. Realizing the café sold more coffee than anything else, it was logical to create it around coffee. "David Dallis, who owned Dallis Bros. coffee roasters in Queens, a third-generation coffee roaster, was a great mentor to us," says Steve. "We wanted to do what he did, and we also wanted a different environment than New York City. So we bought a Victorian farmhouse in Millerton, which was built in 1897 and had been owned by a New York City schoolteacher for about twenty years and was in great disrepair. We bought a 60-kilo roaster from Diedrich Manufacturing in Sandpoint, Idaho, installed it in one of the original carriage houses on the farm, and we were in business."

The original impulse was to create a coffee unlike what one then typically found in the city. Steve and David concluded that coffee in New York was either a too lightly roasted deli coffee or a too dark Italian roast that tasted burnt and bitter. "We decided on a medium roast," he says. "A medium roast coffee with a very heavy body to distinguish it. Of course, we vary the roast depending on the crop or on the various beans within a roast, but basically it has remained the same."

Irving Farms offers about 40 different coffees, which cover all the major growing regions in the world, including several Fair Trade, organic coffees. After an extensive trip to Peru to meet coffee farmers, they added their Rainforest line: 100 percent organic coffees that are shade-grown, fairly traded and certified by the Rainforest Alliance, an organization devoted to the preservation of tropical forests.

The proprietary 71 Irving Place House Blend is a combination of

Nicaraguan and Indonesian beans, which makes a full-bodied, nutty, and softly acidic coffee. The blend used for espresso is a French roast comprised of four different coffees from Guatemala, Brazil, Sumatra, and Java.

Latte art is eschewed. According to Steve Leven, "We simply can't do it. It requires space and time. It would create havoc if we asked our customers to wait another 30 to 40 seconds for their drinks."

Muffin, one of the managers, echoes that assessment. "We're much too busy. Busy even at times of day when other places aren't. Quick and efficient service is what is required. We're like those women in hoop skirts, whose feet are moving like crazy but the effect of them walking is one of calmness. Same here. We try to maintain a calm while moving like crazy."

If providing their own coffee sets 71 Irving Place apart from other cafés, Steve also believes his staff distinguishes it as well. Actors, artists, and students, they have been together a long time. He estimates that three-quarters of them have been there at

least five years. Bill, one of the managers and also a part-time photographer, started at the café's original location at 52 Irving Place ("which was one-sixth the size of No. 71 and one-tenth the rent") and has been with the café ever since.

"The staff don't just work here," Steve explains. "They are part of the community. And people who come here on a regular basis recognize that. I am no longer here very much, nor is David, so the personality of the place is theirs rather than ours... The staff functions as owners. That allows us to concentrate on the coffee."

Although located a stone's throw from the posh environs of the private Gramercy Park, 71 Irving Place is also proximate to, and perhaps more kindred spirit with, the neighborhoods of Union Square, Madison Park, and the Flatiron District. These neighborhoods are filled with professionals (this is the land of non-profit organizations), artists, writers, freelancers of every stripe, "elderly Gramercy Park ladies," slews of young moms and students (NYU and the School of Visual Arts as well as Washington Irving High School are nearby). These groups comprise 71's eclectic customers who often rub shoulders with celebrities who reside in the neighborhood or nearby.

Customers—celebrity or otherwise—are made to feel comfortable in a below street level (four steps down) space with a couple dozen tables. A working fireplace has been restored, though it is never used. That would require removing the two or three tables next to it, which is much needed space. If the café feels a bit crowded— too many tables packed into too little space—it is exactly the feeling its owners intend. "In New York people are so disconnected from each other," Steve says. "Look how close to each other people here have to sit. That's a good thing. We truly bring people together."

One regular customer, a lapsed lawyer now a food writer, tells how she literally was brought together with her present boyfriend. "I met him here last summer," she exclaims. "I've been coming here for ten years. It finally paid off! I might have my wedding here!"

"Really?" Steve Leven asks.

Note: A new location, called Irving Farm Coffee Company (56 Seventh Avenue between 13th and 14th Streets) just opened in the summer of 2007 in the West Village. Subway: 1, 2, 3 to 14th Street.

Short Cups

Not far from Union Square are **Dean & DeLuca Coffee-Tea** (75 University Place between 11th and 12th), a café and not one of their gourmet stores, and **News Café** (107 University Place between 13th and 14th). Also, **Joe, the Art of Coffee** (9 East 13th Street between Fifth Avenue and University Place), though technically in the Village, is still just a stone's throw from Union Square (see page 84).

· 6 ·

CHELSEA

C helsea is a happening neighborhood. Just north of the Village and south of the Garment District—15th Street to about 34th Street, between the Hudson River and Sixth Avenue—Chelsea runneth over with restaurants, bars, shops (including a string of national chains along Sixth Avenue), theaters, cinemas, and galleries. The gallery scene that once dominated SoHo has in recent years relocated to Chelsea, primarily along the blocks west of Tenth Avenue. Chelsea is also the locus of the city's largest—or at least most visible—gay population. Along the Hudson River, much of Chelsea remains industrial, while the blocks between Ninth and Tenth Avenues, from 20th Street to 22nd, boast some of the cities most exquisite brownstones.

Antique Café

234 W. 27th Street
(between 7th and 8th Avenues)
(212) 243-2326
www.antiquecafeny.com
Open 8AM–6PM daily
Subway: A, C, E, F, 1, 2, 3, 9 to 23rd Street

Though the Antique Café, a long and exceedingly narrow sliver of a place, sits in the middle of the one-block-long campus of the Fashion Institute of Technology (FIT), it is hardly a typical campus coffeehouse. It is much more marked by Chelsea's hetero-geneity—the neighborhood borders the Garment District, the Flower District, Greenwich Village, the Meatpacking District, and the massive Penn South Houses—than by its "campus" location.

Antique Café's student patrons comprise perhaps fifty percent of its clientele (a sign in front says discounts are available to FIT students with ID)—more in between classes—but the non-student customers are as varied as the neighborhood and its immediate environs: faculty and administrators, artists from the many nearby studios and loft dwellings, clothing designers, office workers, businessmen and women, neighborhood residents and, also, tourists who may wander in (Penn Station, Madison Square Garden, and Macy's are all within a stone's throw).

One block south, on 26th Street between 7th and 8th Avenues, are the Chelsea Television Studios where the Martha Stewart Show is filmed and where the Ricki

Lake Show used to be. Though Martha herself has not graced the premises, many of the show's staff frequent the Antique Café.

If the regular customers of Antique Café are not typical of other college cafés, neither is its international staff. A Peruvian owner, an Indonesian manager, and wait and counter staff from Mexico, Ecuador, Brazil, Poland, and Hungary. If you need anything translated from almost any foreign language into English, this is the place to go!

Filled with antiques—most notably two beautiful stained glass windows rescued from a church in Brooklyn and a large mirror picked up at an estate sale in Boston—the Antique Café opened at its first location in 1996.

Its owners, Marcial Cavero and Jon Wolohojian, met in the 1990s when both were immersed in the Chelsea antique world. Jon (who has since died) and Marcial were doing their usual weekend antique dealing at the flea market that used to be on Sixth Avenue between 25th and 26th Streets, when Jon said, "You know, there is no place to drink coffee or eat around here. Why don't we start a café?"

Marcial, who had worked in several restaurants since moving to New York as a seventeen-year-old kid from Ica, Peru simply replied, "Okay." They found a small space on West 25th Street and named it the "Antique Café," for the neighborhood's antique houses and flea markets that they dearly loved.

"We were a great partnership," Marcial says. "Jon was an excellent and smart businessman. Aside from having started his own clothing business and later a bed &

breakfast, he had always been creative about food. He had traveled all around the world and knew Korean, Thai, Mediterranean, and South American foods."

"I concentrated on the design of the space," Marcial continues. "Jon created the menu. I kept the books. Jon did our public relations. We were very successful. This was in the pre-Starbucks days. We were selected by the website, Citysearch, as Manhattan's number one café."

But that space was too small, so they sold it and opened a new Antique Café on West 26th Street (see page 106), which was also a success and continues to thrive. Three years later, in February of 2005, they opened the Antique Café on the FIT campus, on the ground floor of a small tenement building from about 1875. It kept many of the same customers and the spirit of the original café. It is, as they say, same pickle, different barrel.

"During those years," says Marcial, "Jon and I learned the magic of having a café— it is about making friends. Jon, who was a workaholic, died at the end of that year at the age of 44. His last words to me were to keep going. He also asked that his mother, Anita Wolohojian, be involved." And Anita is still involved, giving her support, mostly at the West 26th Street location.

Since it was the lack of coffee in the immediate neighborhood that spawned the idea for the Antique Café, it is not surprising that coffee has always figured prominently in the overall operation. "Jon always liked a very strong cup of coffee," says Marcial. We took a full year, testing different coffees, before we settled on our house blend, a combination of Peruvian, African, and Guatemalan beans. It's very strong. Rich in flavor and rich in body."

The beans for their brewed coffee and espresso both come from Eldorado Coffee Roasters in Maspeth, Queens, whose attitude towards coffee is succinctly stated on its website: "Black as hell, strong as death and sweet as love."

In addition to their excellent coffee, Antique Café offers a wide range of baked goods. They make their own croissants, *pain au chocolat*, muffins, and cookies while buying other baked goods and sweets from outside suppliers. They also have an interesting and eclectic range of light foods that reflect Jon Wolohojian's creative flair and knowledge of world cuisines: sandwiches, salads, empanadas, quiches, frittatas, bruschettas, and pastas. At lunch hour, the café is more about the food than the coffee.

It is before or after lunch that customers come to sit in front of the fireplace to relax. During these off-meal times, customers come to study, write, talk, work on their laptops (there is wireless access), read a book, or one of the café's newspapers and magazines (several, not surprisingly, fashion magazines), or play one of the games stored in the bookshelves behind the fireplace.

The many antiques create a homey atmosphere, and thanks to the decidedly not antique, but very modern track lighting, this otherwise dark space shines brightly.

R.I.P. Jon Wolohojian. Antique Café is in good hands and doing just fine.

Note: The other Antique Café location is at 55 West 26th Street (between Sixth Avenue and Broadway). Subway: F to 23rd Street. Although technically Chelsea, this is its far eastern boundary, in a murky area of the city. Maybe Chelsea. Not quite Madison Park. Not quite the Flatiron District. Perhaps Midtown South Central is the most accurate designation.

Though related in spirit and otherwise to the 27th Street location, with staff flowing back and forth, it is the older and wiser cousin. Everything about it is more sophisticated, starting with its space, which occupies the bottom of a new luxury, thirty-story high-rise. It also has a more diverse, less student defined, clientele; a more extensive and varied food menu; a license to serve wine and beer; an outdoor plaza seating area; and quieter music. And it stays open later.

It is, in the words of Anita Wolohojian, who orchestrates much of what goes on at 26th Street, the perfect computer date place. The bench out front allows someone to sit anonymously and check out a possible date even before deciding whether to identify oneself and actually have a cup of coffee. If that goes well, a glass of wine. And, then, if they're getting on famously, they can stay for dinner!

Since the 26th Street location has a smaller indoor space, it can be busier and noisier than the 27th Street Antique Café. At those times, some of the regular customers, who often pinball between both locations, seek out the more relaxed atmosphere of 27th Street.

You choose.

Short Cups

The Big Cup Tea & Coffee House on Eighth Avenue at 22nd Street was the peerless Chelsea gathering place, certainly for gay men, though non-gays were welcome. Unfortunately, the Big Cup closed in the summer of 2005, and nothing quite like it has taken its place. One can rely, however, on the Chelsea locations of three featured cafés from other neighborhoods. They include: **Cupcake Café** at Books of Wonder (18 West 18th Street between Fifth and Sixth Avenues) located inside the children's bookstore (see page 117); **Café Grumpy** (224 West 20th Street between Seventh and Eighth Avenues) which has two Clovers for making single-cup, made-to-order brewed coffee (see page 200); and **Ninth Street Espresso** at Chelsea Market (75 Ninth Avenue between 15th and 16th), the newest location of this East Village icon (see page 65).

· 7 ·

HELL'S KITCHEN

The name Hell's Kitchen conjures a rough-and-tumble past populated by Irish-American mobsters (think Damon Runyon) and Irish and Puerto Rican street gangs (think West Side Story). Others prefer to call the neighborhood Clinton, which fits its more gentrified contemporary state. Running from about 34th Street to 57th Street—though some say from 40th to 59th—between Eighth Avenue and the Hudson River, it is bordered on the north by the Upper West Side and on the south by Chelsea. (During the Clinton presidential years, the Chelsea Clinton News, *a community newspaper serving both neighborhoods, delighted in its name.) Ninth Avenue between 37th and 57th Streets, the location of the city's annual International Food Fesitval, is among the best and most ethnically diverse food venues in Manhattan.*

Cupcake Café

**545 Ninth Avenue
(between 40th and 41st Streets)
(212) 268-9975
www.cupcakecafe.com
Open 7AM–7PM Mon to Fri
8AM–7PM Sat; 9AM–5PM Sun
Subway: A, C, E to 42nd Street/
Port Authority Bus Terminal**

So much for the adage about location, location, location. Despite its somewhat questionable location virtually underneath the tiered roadways leading in and out of the Port Authority Bus Terminal—the Cupcake Café is a veritable New York City institution, known far and wide for its decorative floral cakes and cupcakes, which, in the words of one well-known food writer, "are strewn with bright buttercream blossoms like wildflowers in a meadow." Madonna and Mick Jagger have bought birthday cakes from here.

Rather than rest on its laurels—literally—in the spring of 2004, the Cupcake Café opened Casa Cupcake on 40th Street and Ninth Avenue, a block north across the street from the 39th Street location where it had been for eighteen years. Casa was created to be "an oasis for coffee," and cupcakes were not even served.

But two years later the original Cupcake Café moved into Casa. The two Cupcakes coexist, with the café in front and the bakery in the back.

Strangely, the original impetus for starting the Cupcake Café was not cupcakes, but doughnuts. Mike and Ann Warren, the founders and owners, met working for the Well-Bred Loaf wholesale bakers. The original idea was to reinvent the doughnut,

and the "cup" in Cupcake was really about a cup of coffee. "My suggestion," Mike says, "was to call it 'Cup & Cruller,' but I got shot down."

"We started deep-frying doughnuts in our apartment when the landlady was out," he recalls. "Gradually the doughnut we were seeking evolved—one with a natural shelf-life. Not artificial. We lived from batch to batch. Then we stumbled upon a guy at the Kimberton Community Fair in Pennsylvania where fabulous doughnuts were on sale. He told us the secret of great doughnuts was mashed potatoes, not for flavor but for moisture. This was in 1988. We had just moved into a former Italian bakery we leased on 39th Street and Ninth Avenue. And then sometime in 1989, Molly O'Neill, the food writer for the *Times* wrote an article about doughnuts. Our sales increased from 15 dozen a day to 120 dozen."

Muffins, other breakfast pastries, pies, cakes, and cupcakes followed. Originally the cupcakes were decorated with whipped cream. Ann, who was trained as an artist, later thought of "painting" with buttercream—she is the genius behind the fancifully designed and decorated cakes and cupcakes.

"And once the fashionistas at the time hooked into the cupcake vibe, well, that was it," says Mike.

Adorned with what look like hothouse-quality daisies, sunflowers, zinnias, peonies, dahlias, lilies, irises, violets, lilacs, and more, those cakes and cupcakes have been the Cupcake Café's bread and butter ever since. Or, shall we say, bread and buttercream!

The original Cupcake Café never won any interior design accolades (even its owner admits it was "beyond shopworn its last three years"). Cupcake Café at 40th Street, however, is a feast for the eyes. You don't know where to look first. A reporter once described it as evoking an archaeological dig, with its patches of exposed brick wall and multiple slabs of marble for counters and tabletops. The absolutely gorgeous *piece de resistance*, a four-inch thick slab that seats ten and serves as the café's centerpiece, was salvaged from the sculpture workshop at the Cathedral of St. John the Divine on the Upper West Side.

The café is now filled with antiques and just plain old tchotchkes: ovens, wooden iceboxes, a cash register, cabinets, pews, a cider press, a piano, and an humongous mirrored bar from someplace in Pennsylvania, not to mention a yellow $10,000 Aga stove, which serves as a coffee stand! Archaeological dig meets estate sale.

This mix of styles and objects works. A unifying calm and warmth pervades, particularly in the front near the window that stretches across the width of the café. A part-time musician and book editor who patronizes the café daily, says, "It's beautiful. It's funky. The light is wonderful. And I love this table [the four-inch wide marble slab]. I always want to sit at this table because… I don't know. It's just *so* beautiful."

The La Marzocco FB70 two-group espresso machine, with its bright red metallic high-performance sports car finish, makes clear that this place is serious about its coffee.

"I never would have anticipated Mike becoming a coffee guy," says a managing partner for La Colombe Torrefaction, the boutique coffee roasting company in Philadelphia that provides Cupcake's coffee. "But he has."

Not only has Mike Warren become a coffee guy, but he seems invigorated by the label after so many years of being known as the cupcake guy. "Doug Zell from Intelligentsia Coffee in Chicago was in here and had an espresso. He said it was a better shot than the espresso pulled at La Colombe's own café in Philadelphia! Another customer, a guy from Seattle, said our coffee was on a par with Café Victrola out there." (Both Intelligentsia and Café Victrola are coffee roasters and cafés who by consensus pretty much set the standard for specialty coffees.)

Cupcake uses a medium dark roast for its brewed coffee, and Colombe's Nizza blend, a soft dark roast, for its espresso. Made up of five different beans—mostly from South and Central America—all Arabica and all organic, it has a caramel taste, more delicate than most dark roasts.

The baristas at the Cupcake have helped establish and then maintain the high quality of the coffee. First there was Andrew—or Andrew the English guy as most every-one refers to him—a maestro who has since returned to his native England.

Other baristas at the Cupcake Café are spoken of fondly and admiringly by customers. As one regular patron describes them, "There was Andrew from England who was a real coffee guy. And then there was the scruffy, lanky rock and roll musician. The stage director. The random Scotsman. The dancer. Basically, every ridiculous hopeless performance artist you could imagine. They were all great."

Though tourists come seeking the famous cakes, and others come from all over the New York metropolitan area for the baked goods, it is the regular locals who give the place its character and soul. The daily cast of characters includes the freelance musician and

book editor who loves the marble slab, the older theater gentleman, the non-linear food caterer, the opera singer who wears sandals, the composer, the concierge, the event planner, and the IT guy, to name some of the hardcore.

All of these regulars express great affection for the café. "Two things changed my life in New York," says the composer. "First, Hudson River Park, which I walk almost every day. Second, this place. This café. It's authentic. And the coffee is great. Every cup is made with care. Every bean chosen with care. And the people who hang out and congregate here are interesting. Where else could I have a conversation about an important, esoteric aspect of composition? And Mike's a great friend. He knows literature and theater. He knows what's going on in the world and the city." (Mike, who's nearing 60, was an English literature major at Columbia.)

"During the last World Cup Soccer Tournament, Mike turned all the pews around to face the wall on which he installed a television. It was like stadium seating in here. The place was packed everyday. We called it 'The World Cupcake Café.' I'm amazed that people go to Starbucks instead."

"I come here, of course, for the coffee," explains the freelance musician and book editor. "There is a totally new level of espresso-ness here. Often I'm in my face-in-the-newspaper mode. But when I am in the mood, I can have the most interesting conversations here. I call it 'intellectual riffing.' There's the the guy I call 'the non-linear food caterer.' And Mike is non-linear. You kind of have to have your batteries in to follow how their minds work. But if you do, it's fascinating."

To fully appreciate the Cupcake Café's coffee and colorful cast of characters, you should probably come often and stay for a long time.

Note: The Cupcake Café branch at the children's bookstore Books of Wonder opened in January of 2005 in the Chelsea/Flatiron District of Manhattan. 18 West 18th Street (between Fifth and Sixth Avenues). Subway: F, V, L to 14th Street/Union Sq.

Not surprisingly, the look is unlike adult-centered cafés: ladybugs are painted on tables and chairs. Its primary customers are the kids and their parents who come to the bookstore. All of which is to say, this is not really a neighborhood gathering place, however wonderful the fanciful cakes, coffee, and other food served is. This is not quite the daily place that the 40th Street and Ninth Avenue location is (unless one buys children's books on a daily basis), but some people who work in the neighborhood have figured out it's a great everyday place to go for lunch. The soups in particular are good, and most kids are in school!

Short Cups

Less a residential neighborhood than many other parts of Manhattan, it is not surprising that Hell's Kitchen does not have a plethora of neighborhood cafés. There is **The Coffee Pot** (327 West 49th Street at Ninth Avenue), and although primarily a coffee roaster/wholesaler/retailer, **Empire Coffee & Tea Company** (568 Ninth Avenue at 49th Street)—founded in 1908!—does have a chair, a couch, a bench, and three stools to create a small, in-store café. And in early summer 2007, **Bis.Co. Latte** (667 Tenth Avenue between 46th and 47th Streets) opened, offering 20 flavors of their own baked biscottis along with teas, coffee, and chocolate drinks.

· 8 ·

❧

UPPER EAST SIDE

Stretching from 59th to 96th Street, between Central Park and the East River, the Upper East Side is blessed with the city's greatest concentration of museums—the Metropolitan, Guggenheim, Whitney, Frick, and Cooper-Hewitt among them. The neighborhood has long been thought of as the city's wealthiest enclave, and apartments along Fifth and Park Avenues, or townhouses on the cross streets in the 60s and 70s are certainly the domain of investment bankers who earn multimillion dollar bonuses. Rupert Murdoch, the media mogul, bought his apartment on Fifth Avenue at 65th Street for $44 million in 2004, then a city record.

Java Girl

348 East 66th Street
(between First & Second Avenues)
(212) 737-3490
www.javagirl.com
Open 6:30AM–7PM Mon to Fri
8:30AM–6PM Sat & Sun
Subway: F to 63rd Street; 6 to
68th Street

*W*ho would expect to find a friendly, spirited café the size of a shoe box on the Upper East Side? A place whose eclectic decor might even qualify it as funky. After all, the Upper East Side is not exactly known for its funk. Toniness rather than funkiness is more in keeping with this generally wealthy and upscale neighborhood.

Java Girl is located on a modest, unassuming block (for the Upper East Side, that is) of mostly older, small, walk-up apartment buildings (you can tell them by the fire escapes attached to the façades) sprinkled with commercial establishments on the same small scale: a shoe repair shop, a dry cleaners, a tailor, and a Japanese restaurant. And, oh yes, a Dunkin' Donuts on the corner, which for some inexplicable reason has increased Java Girl's business rather than competed with it. "I guess," says Linda Rizzuto, Java Girl's owner and guiding spirit, "it's a case of someone coming upon the Dunkin' Donuts and saying, 'Oh no, is this the only place around here where I can get a cup of coffee?' And so they look for an alternative. I'm that alternative!"

Linda opened Java Girl in the fall of 1998, although the "Java Girl" of the café's logo was created years earlier, before she had any idea she would have a café. "I had always been artistic, but I hadn't drawn for a number of years. But right after my divorce, I began to draw again, and one of the first drawings I did was of this woman who for me symbolized power, dignity, and respect. I decided right then that whatever business I started, that woman figure would represent it. She would be the logo.

"So when I opened the café," she continues, "I needed a name for her. She became 'Java Girl!' I thought maybe it was too goofy or too juvenile, but it has turned out to be a lot of fun, and the name has been very well received."

The impetus to start Java Girl grew out of Linda's dissatisfactions with the corporate world in which she worked for a dozen years in the field of visual merchandising and store design. Although she was good at what she did—so good that she traveled around the country to train

others—she was not enamored of the corporate environment. "Basically, I was afraid I would become like the people I worked for… I had a vision to start a place where people did not have to talk about work. Where they could take a breath, get away from the heaviness of their work. A place just to be."

Although Java Girl is undeniably a café, Linda tries not to refer to it as such. "'Everything is a café today," she maintains. "It's been stomped over. I prefer to call this a coffee shop or coffeehouse, like the original coffeehouses where the main focus was as a community gathering place, where people came to talk about issues."

The smallness of the place— half of which is devoted to the sale of coffees, teas, and related paraphernalia, and half to café seating—dictates not only its ambiance but also the dynamics of what transpires, and how. There are a small number of tables with not much space between them, and some bench seating out front. But when the café is crowded—three would not a crowd make, but ten might!—the ethos of the place is such that one shares tables. "If you're not that kind of person, then you won't like it here," declares Linda. "It's just too small. The Starbucks crowd with their laptops and such, and papers spread out over two tables, would not be comfortable here. Nor would it work. This is a community place. Not one's office or dorm room. Ninety-percent of the people who come here are wonderful. They are the sharing sort."

Being the community-based coffeehouse that it is, Java Girl has a clientele that reflects that community. "It's a very eclectic group of people… people who live in fancy buildings west of here and people who live in the tenements east of here. And with so many hospitals being nearby, we get lots of scientists." (York Avenue throughout the East 60s has so many hospitals along its stretch that it is often referred to as "Bedpan Alley.")

"We don't get that many doctors, because they don't normally have the time to just cut out. But rather we get scientists who work in the labs. At a certain point, they have to leave their experiments, so they come here. We had a group from a lab at Rockefeller University come here every afternoon for three years. They'd come here to decompress while their experiments were being run. And guess what? The head of the lab wound up winning the Nobel Prize for Medicine! The entire lab came here afterwards to celebrate. That was wonderful. Just incredible."

According to Linda, the patrons are split 50/50 politically. "We get staunch conservatives and staunch liberals. Not too many in between, which means when it comes to politics, things can get quite heated, which is why I try to keep it low key."

Watch Linda pour ungodly quantities of sugar into the cup of coffee she pours for herself, and one could easily jump to the conclusion that she pays little attention to the quality of coffee. Quite the contrary. "I feel strongly about coffee," she says emphatically. Sugar in her own coffee is apparently just a bad habit of hers, going back to her youth. Smoking too. "Although I do other things—soups, pressed sandwiches, salads, yogurt, rice pudding, fresh juices—coffee is the heart of the business. In the future, I would like to do more with tea, but up to now, the focus has been on coffee."

"I could have easily substituted a cheaper coffee, but I won't. I've always used the same coffees. White House coffees from White Coffee Corporation in Long Island City," she says. "Actually, the same place the gourmet grocery that was here before me used. They are very high quality. Third generation-run. No one can match their flavored coffees; all natural flavors. No chemicals."

The house coffee, served daily, is a strong French Roast Mexican Altura. A different milder alternative is offered every day. It might be a Mocha Java or a Kenyan coffee (she is a big fan of African coffees, liking their high acidity and the resulting sharpness) or a blend called Tip of the Andes. The decaf is always a medium roast, either Mocha Java or Colombian. And for espresso, she uses Danesi espresso.

Expect to drink a very high quality cup of coffee at Java Girl, or buy a pound of high quality coffee from more than forty different kinds sold, or have one blended to your individual taste and specifications. If you come across a drink you have never heard of before, don't worry. It is not your lack of knowledge—it just means that one of Java Girl's staff has concocted a drink ($100 bonus if it catches on). Antonio's Mint Mocha is such a drink.

"Soon after I opened, some people who had lived in the same building for years but had never met, finally met here in my café. I liked the fact that my space brought them together and that they would no longer continue to be strangers… It's a community here, a family. People need help, a place to go."

"And, ah yes, the babies. I love seeing a newborn baby from the neighborhood, and then getting a hug from that baby a couple of years later. That's when," she says, "I know I am in the right place."

Short Cups

The closer one gets to Madison Avenue stores, Fifth Avenue museums, or Central Park, the more likely one is to find cafés frequented primarily by tourists and visitors. For more neighborhood type cafés, stay east—Lexington Avenue or beyond. There is **M. Rohr's House of Fine Teas and Coffees** (303 East 85th Street at Second Avenue), a century-old tea and coffee purveyor. With some comfy, lived-in seating on its premises, it is a small—very small—café as well. Also, **Sicaffe** (964 Lexington Avenue between 70th and 71st) actually does its own coffee roasting in the back of the café.

· 9 ·

UPPER WEST SIDE/
MORNINGSIDE HEIGHTS

The Upper West Side is sometimes referred to as the "Upper Left Side" because of its erstwhile reputation as home to progressive New Yorkers, to intellectuals, to makers of culture. For a long time, if one subscribed to Lenny Bruce's dichotomy, defining things as either goyish or Jewish—the Upper East Side was goyish and the Upper West Side Jewish. But New York never remains the same, and as real estate prices on the West Side came in many instances to surpass those on the East Side, other distinctions blurred. Between the Hudson River to Central Park, the Upper West Side runs from 59th to 110th Street. From 110th to 125th Street is Morningside Heights, with the ever-expanding Columbia University as its centerpiece.

The Hungarian Pastry Shop

**1030 Amsterdam Avenue
(between West 110th & 111th
Streets)
(212) 866-4230
Open 7:30AM–11:30PM Mon to Fri
8:30AM–11:30PM Sat; 8:30AM–
10:30PM Sun
Subway: 1, 9 to 110th Street**

The sign next to the coffee pot on top of the counter says "Help Yourself to Free Refills." It is true. Once you pay for that first cup of coffee, unlimited refills are free. The message is clear. Make yourself at home. Stay as long as you want!

Most customers take that message to heart and do stay, so finding a table at this always crowded Upper West Side storefront pastry shop/café, the first floor of an apartment building, may seem daunting. But even if a table to yourself is not always available, a free seat or two almost always is, which means you might sit elbow to elbow between people who may no longer be strangers by the time you leave. In any case, the tables are so close together that a table to yourself is hardly that, a feature that this café somehow turns into an asset rather than a liability.

If cafés in New York can be broken down into those whose focus is the coffee and those whose central concern is the atmosphere, there is no doubt the Hungarian Pastry Shop, or the HPS as some regulars fondly refer to it, falls into the "atmosphere" category. In fact, it probably reigns at the top of that list—despite its good coffee and espresso, made with a high quality Colombia bean, and the often excellent pastries: the rigo, dobos, hamantash, and four kinds of strudel among the most popular. (It might be the only place left in the city to get authentic Hungarian sour cherry strudel.)

But in the words of one customer who has been coming for over 25 years, sometimes six or seven days a week, "The pastry is almost secondary. I come here for the ambiance. There are always interesting people here, a real mix of races and nationalities. I came here after moving to New York from Armenia and it was love at first sight. I had always been a café person and was looking for the kind of café that was about socializing and communicating; a café where you came for inspiration, to learn something, or hear something that didn't come from newspapers or TV or books." (In fact, once he discovered the HPS, he moved to be within walking distance!)

Founded in 1961 by an Hungarian couple—both bakers—the HPS has been at this same location ever since, no mean feat given the rapacious Manhattan real estate market, particularly in this ultra-gentrified Columbia University neighborhood. To accomplish this longevity without owning the building is a veritable miracle.

Panagiotis Binioris, often called Peter, bought the café from the original owners in 1976 and has protected their legacy of an Old World European style café ever since. "I grew up in the Peloponnese region of Greece and had two uncles who owned cafés… Cafés where you could just have a glass of water and stay forever. That is what I knew and what I was nostalgic for once I arrived in New York in 1970."

The opportunity to replicate that vision of European café life came while he was working as a waiter at the Symposium Greek restaurant on 113th Street, just up and around the corner from the HPS. His boss at the time, Yanni Posnakoff, lived above the Hungarian Pastry Shop, and was a neighbor and friend of the Hungarian couple. When they decided to sell, they asked Yanni if he wanted to buy. He recruited Panagiotis to be his partner. And that is the partial explanation for how a Greek café in New York City comes to feature Hungarian pastry! (Yanni has long since returned to Greece, though his paintings and his Greek-style lettering on the walls remain.)

"I didn't want to change anything," Panagiotis says. "I liked it the way it was and wanted to maintain the tradition. They gave us their recipes, so we served the same pastries, with only a few things added, like croissants. But aside from opening up the space, taking down the wall that divided the place into two separate rooms, I've kept everything the same. Oh, yes—I added tables on the sidewalk, the first place in the area to do so. I wanted to make it more like the cafés of my native Greece. I didn't even know you needed a license for it! But otherwise, I've kept everything the same." As though it were a warmer climate, people actually use the outdoor seating year round.

The HPS has proved its staying power, and after 40 years, it has achieved the status of institution. For anyone who has ever spent any substantial time above 79th Street, it is a well-known place. Woody Allen featured it in his film *Husbands and Wives*, in an establishing shot to identify this particular Upper West Side neighborhood. The dust jacket blurb for Jenny McPhee's 2004 novel *No Ordinary Matter*, says, "The sisters meet monthly at the Hungarian Pastry Shop, where they entangle their futures and unravel their pasts…" and instantly establishes a sense of place. Mention the HPS to anyone who has ever spent more than a semester at Columbia or Barnard and there will be immediate recognition and reminiscence.

Depending upon when you come, the HPS can seem dominated by students. But they are only part of the picture. There has always been a contingent of loyal neighborhood customers and a regular influx of tourists who come to visit the Cathedral of St. John the Divine, the world's largest gothic cathedral (it's roughly the length of two football fields!) across the street.

That the Hungarian Pastry Shop has never morphed into your garden variety, heavily trafficked, fill'em and spill'em dessert café—like most of the myriad such cafés that have always dotted the Upper West Side—is testament to Panagiotis's commitment to the original vision. But that he has been able to maintain the HPS as a European style café certainly owes something to its proximity to Columbia. Students and academics have made for a customer base that likes to hang out, study, write, read, and—above all else—talk.

And talk they do. Like any other café these days, there are always a certain number of laptops, but the wonderful thing about the HPS is that despite its large academic patronage, there is always more social activity than computer activity. Perhaps it has something to do with the lack of electrical outlets and Wi-Fi, but it probably has more to do with Panagiotis's social ethos, which is more in tune with the early coffeehouse tradition where talk and the exchange of ideas was central.

Indeed, conversation—far more so than the pastry or coffee—is the defining trait of the HPS. And what conversation it is! Politics. Literature. Politics. Love. Politics. Art. Philosophy. Politics. Film. Politics. Yes, politics more than anything, and politics of a decidedly left persuasion. (The *Village Voice* not long ago voted it "Best Geopolitical Coffeehouse Graffiti," and so it is. A sampling from the restroom walls: "We learn from history that we do not learn from history."—Hegel. "To talk about the ineffable is to say practically nothing at all." "Love makes the time pass. Time makes the love pass.")

The inherent magic of the HPS is that somehow one is able to carry on a conversation, comfortably and in a normal speaking voice, while at the same time eavesdropping on the conversations of others. And this acoustical magic works in such a way that the din of constant chatter somehow creates an atmosphere of stillness, almost like white noise, and a feeling of peace and quiet prevails. The calm of the Hungarian Pastry Shop *is* the storm. And that is magic.

Lest anyone fear this magic might disappear anytime soon, take heart, for Panagiotis has both a long lease and large family. His wife Wendy, whom he met when she was a waitress at the HPS, and their four children all work here. And, Panagiotis assures people that HPS will stay in the family. And that it will remain the same.

As always.

Short Cups

One would think the Upper West Side would be rife with independently owned neighborhood cafés. Its residential population would certainly support them, as it does the many Starbucks that fill the neighborhood café void (or create it, whichever the case may be). In fact, the first Starbucks to open in Manhattan was on the Upper West Side. But the high cost of space on its major commercial strips proscribes cafés that are not driven by the imperatives of high volume and high turnover. Thus, although there are scores of places on the Upper West Side to have coffee, they are of the Starbucks corporate ilk, or they are places that call themselves "cafés" but in actuality are something else. Alas, the Hungarian Pastry Shop stands out as one of a kind.

· 10 ·

HARLEM

Spanning the width of Manhattan from the Hudson River to the East River, with 155th Street as its northern boundary, Harlem at its south boundary is less linear: 125th Street in West Harlem, 110th Street in Central Harlem, and 96th Street in East (or Spanish) Harlem. Once defined by Ralph Ellison as "anywhere uptown where blacks live," Harlem has long been the center of African-American life, most famously in the 1920s, when black literature, music, and art flourished. Thanks to a housing stock that includes some amazingly beautiful buildings (Strivers Row, 138th and 139th Street between Seventh and Eighth Avenues, for example), today Harlem has attracted a new generation of young professional renters and owners of all races.

Society Coffee Lounge

2104 Frederick Douglass Blvd.
(at 114th Street)
(212) 222-3323
www.societycoffee.com
Open 12PM–10PM Mon
9AM–10PM Tues to Thurs
9AM–midnight Fri & Sat
9AM–9PM Sun
Subway: B, C to 116th Street

Society Coffee Lounge, a fashionable yet laid-back café and wine bar in Harlem is greater—or, certainly, different—than the sum of its parts. Consider the mix: One thirty-something dreadlocked African-American owner with an engineering degree from Yale and a Polish-German manager (a lapsed lawyer) who grew up in Europe, Africa, and Asia. Find a location on the corner of what was once one of the city's roughest blocks in a now gentrifying neighborhood. Include a multiracial, multiethnic staff of models, artists, singers, and one filmmaker whose ambition is to make a feature-length movie in a single day using 66 cameras. Spend $350,000 on renovations, mix good taste with an eye for style and comfort. Add passion for great coffee, fine wine, and good food, and let everything settle around two great square wooden communal tables. Voilá!—there you have it. Society Coffee.

The logo on the front door, "Society, Harlem, NY," trumpets loud and clear that this café is very much about a sense of place. The pride of place is palpable.

When Karl Franz Williams, Society's owner (whose day job is working for Pepsi as brand manager for Mountain Dew), decided to move back to New York in 2001 after living and working in Puerto Rico for two years, he chose to live in Harlem. "I wanted to be in a dynamic neighborhood. One that was on the verge," he says. "I wanted to be in a place, where if I had an idea, I could make it happen. I saw huge opportunity in Harlem. It has great history for black Americans. And I saw a lot of beauty here too. The buildings. The people. The parks. Urban but suburban. I call Harlem the suburbs of Manhattan."

While living in Puerto Rico, he had toyed with the idea of starting a coffeehouse. (He started a dot-com instead.) "I knew I wanted to do something. I just wasn't sure what. But when I moved to Harlem, I realized there weren't a lot of cool, everyday places around. I found myself running down to Starbucks at Astor Place or in SoHo to sit and drink coffee and hang out. I went there every Sunday."

Tom Kurlus, the former lawyer who is now Society's manager, adds, "Not only were there no cafés like this around, there was nothing here at the time. Hardly any businesses of any kind. Not that many people living here. All this new construction you see has been built in the last five years. Back then you could rent an apartment for $400 to $900 a month. Now it's jumped to $1,500 a month." (Posh Paws, the high end pet boutique across the street, is an indicator of just how much the neighborhood has changed in recent years.)

"In any case," Karl Franz continues, "since I had already done some research about starting a café when I was still in Puerto Rico, I knew something about it. And then I decided it was what the neighborhood really needed... I had been reading and thinking about coffee at the time, and I was trying to put into words what coffee, and drinking coffee, was about and what it meant to me... I came up with what is now written on the back of our menus and on our website:

> Café society is about people meeting, thinking, writing, talking and watching—or simply sitting in amiable surroundings with the company or a cup of coffee and a slice of cake, taking time out, in sips.

"The idea of 'life in sips' encapsulated my point of view."

The original plan was to be a coffee and juice bar. To serve something hot in cold weather and something cold when it was warm. But the focus soon moved from juice to wine (though they do serve smoothies), because, as Karl Franz puts it, "People vibe around wine in the same way they do around coffee."

When it opened in June 2005, Society was a coffee bar by day and a wine bar by night. As soon as it became clear that coffee was the café's best seller, baked goods were added. The muffins, cookies, croissants, strudel, and scones are baked on the premises while more complicated sweets, such as the jelly-filled pastries, are prepared by a local Harlem baker, who uses only healthy, high-quality ingredients.

Later, customers asked for a breakfast menu, since few places in the area offered it. Now breakfast is offered every day, all day, and on weekends is a main draw (their chocolate and fruit waffles are in great demand). Next, lunch came along: salads, soups, panini, sandwiches, thin crust pizza, hummus and dip, cheese plates, fondues. "We've tripled the menu since we first opened," says Karl Franz.

"You really shouldn't have food in a coffeehouse," says Tom, the manager, "but it's what the neighborhood wants and needs. Also, given the high rents and other costs of doing business in New York, it is too hard to survive by serving coffee only."

"But," Karl Franz is quick to interject, "coffee is still the cornerstone. Before we opened, I went to a meeting of the Specialty Coffee Association of America and met the head buyer for Fresh Direct. He gave me a crash course in coffee. Then I went around and tasted the coffee of every roaster in the Metropolitan area before I settled on Kobricks in Jersey City."

All of the coffees are provided by Kobricks with the exception of the Rasta Blend, a Jamaican Blue Mountain combined with an Ethiopian Sidamo, which comes from Reggie Roast, also in New Jersey. The most popular brewed coffee is what Society calls their Danube Kaffee, a blend of three coffees, from Costa Rica, Sumatra, and Kenya.

The coffee used to make espresso is Antica Tostatura Triestina, a wood-roasted blend that Kobricks imports from Trieste, Italy. Every two or three weeks Society offers a different flavored coffee—Cinnamon Sticky Bun, anyone?

Sitting at one of the communal tables on a Saturday morning, working at his laptop, Karl Franz looks out onto his open and airy space, and with great satisfaction acknowledges the typically eclectic mix of customers.

"I'm most proud of Society's diversity," he says smiling. "It is the most diverse place in Harlem. Every race. Every sexuality. Staff and customers We're all part of a family. Staff and customers become friends There is just a certain comfort level that everyone has."

"It's racially very mixed," Tom adds, also with pride. "Blacks, Latinos, whites, and lots of Asians. We were even featured in the Japanese edition of GQ!... It's nicer looking than your average place in terms of its design, but it's not overwhelming... pretty much everyone can feel comfortable here."

And everyone seems to. Neighborhood residents. People who work nearby. People who travel to Society from elsewhere in the city, particularly on weekends. Artists, writers, photographers (whose promotional materials are on a table near the front door). Loads of musicians (much of the music played at Society is from cds that musician customers have made). And because the immediate neighborhood is populated with a plethora of schools (Columbia to the west on the other side of Morningside Park as well as several public elementary, middle, and high schools—

including the aptly named Sojourner Truth School), scores of teachers and students are among its regular customers.

   On a random Tuesday afternoon, a group of high school girls spent virtually the entire afternoon at one of the large tables studying and doing homework. Physics, English, and trigonometry books spread out across the table. Reading. Writing. Listening to the upbeat reggae over the sound system (morning music is mellower, more jazz). Nursing a single cup of coffee. And as the afternoon dragged on, munching surreptitiously from a box of Cheez-its brought in from the deli across the street. No one bothering them the entire time.

Yep, one of Harlem's hippest, coolest venues, used as a place to do physics homework! A place where everyone—truly, everyone—can feel comfortable.

Short Cups

Closer to Columbia University than Society Coffee, **Saurin Parke Café** (301 W. 110th Street at Frederick Douglas Blvd.) tends to gets lots of Columbia students, which also means lots of laptop activity. Further east is the **Harlem Tea Room** (1793A Madison Avenue at 118th Street).

11

DUMBO

DUMBO, Down Under the Manhattan Bridge Overpass, is indeed down under the Manhattan Bridge; specifically, stretching along the East River between the Brooklyn and Manhattan Bridge. It is as close to Manhattan as one can get without being in the water. The neighborhood boasts some extraordinary views of the East River, the Manhattan skyline, and the Brooklyn Bridge. A rapidly changing neighborhood that is becoming more residential by the day—though plenty of industrial and artistic activity remains—DUMBO is a bit of old and new New York. Pre–Civil War era warehouse buildings and cobblestone streets co-exist in dramatic proximity with newly renovated multimillion dollar lofts and new 30-story high-rise buildings.

Dumbo General Store

111 Front Street
(between Washington and Adams Streets)
(212) 855-5288
Open 7:30AM–8PM Mon to Wed
7:30AM–late night Thurs to Sat
8:30AM–8PM Sun
Subway: F to York Street; A, C to
High Street-Brooklyn Bridge

*I*f there were no other reason to visit DUMBO General Store aside from the excuse to visit this exciting neighborhood of heavy industry and commerce, artists and artisans, studios and galleries, newly built luxury high-rise apartments, pre-Civil War era buildings, new fine food places and the most exquisite views of the Brooklyn Bridge, East River, and lower Manhattan skyline imaginable, that would be reason enough. And, of course, the Jacques Torres chocolates. As it happens, DUMBO General offers many more reasons and pleasures.

As its name implies, DUMBO General did not start out to be a café: It evolved into one. People came, so Anna Castellani, the founder and owner, made a café.

Anna discovered the neighborhood through her boyfriend (now husband), an artist who was living and working in DUMBO. After returning to New York from a three-and-a-half year stint in Los Angeles as a camera assistant ("physically I was not up to

the challenge," she says of her experience of those pre-digital, heavyweight cameras), she started spending lots of time in this then rather rough, just-starting-to-be gentrified area.

"What I realized," she says of the neighborhood in the year 2000, "is there was absolutely nothing down here. No place to get anything. I took a ten-year lease on this space, not knowing what I was going to do with it. The building's owner reminded me that there was no substantial resident community down here and predicted I would not last a year.

"I decided to open an art supply store to address the needs of the artists—mostly painters—who were working here… But among the many things the neighborhood lacked at the time," she continues, "was a place to get a really good cup of coffee. There was no place, not even in the Heights. I was desperate for good coffee. So, when I opened the store, I put in an espresso machine just to please me. But once that machine was in, it was on fire. Customers would join me for coffee, and soon I realized the store was packed with people. There would be a cacophony of noise. People in overalls covered with paint just standing around drinking coffee, talking, laughing, having a great time.

"DUMBO was still a neighborhood popu-lated by mostly self- employed people—metal workers, woodworkers, artists, architects. Folks with flexible schedules and apparently time to spare. People who seemed desperate for a nice place to go. So we put in electrical coil wheels for tables, got some folding chairs, and before you knew it, we were an art supply store *and* café!"

Since then, the café at DUMBO General has greatly expanded—conceptually and physically—while the art supply store was reduced and ultimately eliminated. (After Anna's own store closed, a SoHo-based art supply store occupied the space for a year and a half or so before it too closed. According to Anna, neither store addressed the needs of the newer multimedia artists who have been replacing the previous generation of artists who were mostly painters.)

The kitchen offerings now include a breakfast menu as well as muffins and pastry from Blue Sky in Park Slope and Baked in Red Hook. From lunch on, there is an abundance of salads and panini (made with ciabattas from Caputo's Bakery in Carroll Gardens). The electrical coil wheels and folding chairs have been replaced with about a half dozen small tables and two very large, long communal tables, with matching chairs, including high-back upholstered armchairs in a seating area surrounding a coffee table. A spiffy bar along with a credible wine list has also been added.

The present space is large, bright, and airy. The ceilings are at least fifteen feet high, and the massive mirrors on opposite walls add to the feeling of spaciousness. The exposed pipes and wires and original cement floor ("we had to remove at least a foot thick mass of tar, asphalt, auto fuel, you name it") speak of the building's industrial past. Still, the space is warm and inviting. Plants and music soften the space. The sound is mellow and upbeat, though Anna admits that she does battle with the young staff over what gets played. "Sometimes it does get too singer-songwriter, but never heavy metal." (There are music events in the evenings from time to time which, unlike the poetry events of the past, have been quite successful.)

The good cup of coffee that ultimately transformed the art supply store into a café is still very much front and center. Believing that it doesn't get better than Italian coffee, DUMBO General uses Danesi for its brewed coffee and espresso. Nearly all the beans are Arabica, but with a little shot of Robusta, as opposed to the more typical 100% Arabica. Also, believing that Italians use milk with less fat than the majority of milk sold in the United States, Anna tried four different milk companies before finding the best milk for steaming.

She herself can do latte art, though she doesn't think a big deal should be made of it. In fact, she pooh-poohs the "Seattle thing"—obsessive attention to coffee that she thinks borders on the precious. "Super-sensitive people sitting around drinking coffee, writing novels, and talking about coffee beans. Too touchy-feely. I like it rougher. More Parisian."

Reminiscing about the early years, from 2000 to 2003—before the real furniture replaced the makeshift stuff and before the walls got painted—Anna says she was blessed. "There was just the right energy mix. The place was always filled with the local artists and local factory workers. The funniest people," she says. "Just great people. It seemed like just one big sweaty mass of mankind. All these straight guys. Sometimes days would pass without a woman customer. The female bar staff I had then would never leave. They were just thrilled to be here, around all these hunky guys.

"The neighborhood's changed now. Just in the past few years. It's a more mainstream, corporate environment. Parts of Manhattan are more affordable than DUMBO! I knew the neighborhood was changing when Starbucks opened up… no one seemed upset about it coming into the neighborhood. No one fought it.

"In the early days, the first three years or so, customers would come in and bus their own dishes. Even wash them! Sometimes they'd take dishes out with them, back to their studios, and then return them. Days later. But they always did. The customers are different now, since the neighborhood is different. And there are tourists who come to see the new, hip DUMBO. It's no accident that we lease out some of our space now to someone selling Danish modern accessories!" (A Scandinavian home goods store now occupies a small space in the back of the café. And on Thursday through Saturday evenings, there is Hecho en DUMBO, an evening of Mexican antojitos—think Spanish tapas—and music.)

The challenge now, as Anna sees it, is for the café to evolve to address the needs of the evolving neighborhood. "I love seeing people walk out the door happy after having entertained them… I still want to do that even though the customers are different now."

"In short," she continues, "I still want to create a fun social environment for myself and for people who come here… I'll just have to do things better. Find professional baristas. Also, get myself back in the kitchen, which is really where I love to be. New furniture. Paint again. Renovate the bar for the fifth time. In other words, adapt to the new DUMBO without losing the purpose or heart and soul of the old."

"And, always, serve a good cup of coffee!"

Short Cups

Coffee Bar at Retreat (147 Front Street at Jay) is located in a small space that is literally a stairwell, but, oh, that fabulous upstairs lounge with free Wi-Fi and lovely terra cotta vaulted ceilings. And just up from DUMBO, on the northern edge of Brooklyn Heights is **Uncommon Grounds Brooklyn** (50 Henry Street at Cranberry).

12

BOERUM HILL / COBBLE HILL

Once referred to by realtors as "Brooklyn Heights Vicinity," these adjoining South Brooklyn neighborhoods no longer need to ride on the coattails of their more chichi neighbor just to the north and west, on the other side of Atlantic Avenue. Nowadays these two brownstone Brooklyn neighborhoods warrant their own billing. Characterized by lovely late 19th-century townhouses, Boerum Hill and Cobble Hill are close enough to Manhattan to be considered almost within walking distance, albeit a very long walk (across the Brooklyn Bridge). Eminently welcoming to both singles and families, in recent years this section of Brooklyn has become a New York City culinary destination, with Smith Street, from Atlantic Avenue on south, at its center.

Boerum Hill Food Company

134 Smith Street
(between Bergen and Dean Streets)
(718) 222-0140
Open 8AM–10PM daily
Subway: F, G to Bergen Street

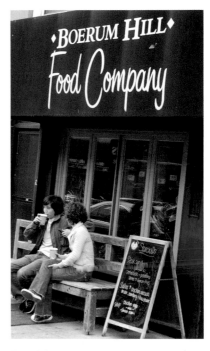

Boerum Hill Food Company—more coffee-house or restaurant? That is the question. Some use it strictly as a place to eat—breakfast, brunch, lunch, and dinner—while others use it for coffee and a place to meet, work, linger. Still others use it as a restaurant *and* a café, a veritable home and office away from home.

When asked one morning to say how she thought of the Food Company, a relative newcomer replied, "Well, I guess it is a restaurant. *But* it has a coffeehouse vibe."

Ultimately, if a place feels like a coffeehouse, sounds like a coffeehouse, and smells like a coffeehouse, well, then it must be one.

At least as far as the daily customers are concerned, it is the café within the restaurant that beckons. They come for coffee and to hang out—almost never for a meal. They patronize it as a café, where they can order a cup of coffee (the refills are free), stay for as long as they want, and never feel as though they've overstayed their welcome.

The story goes that a guy once came in for breakfast, remained for lunch, stayed through dinner, and hung around after that. In between meals he plied himself with coffee, read, worked at his computer, talked with customers, and kibitzed with staff.

Boerum Hill Food Company is that kind of place. Especially if you manage to get one of the two coveted armchairs by the window. At certain times of day, they're drenched in sunlight, at which point inertia becomes a most delicious and powerful force. You could stay until… well, until the next solar eclipse! And the staff would let you. As one staff person has observed, "This is not a place for people who are in a rush."

The Boerum Hill Food Company is on a busy commercial street smack dab in the middle of a family-friendly neighborhood. Saul Bolton, who bought it from the original owners in 2000, is also the owner of the highly regarded restaurant Saul, which is three doors down and consistently among the highest Zagat rated restaurants in Brooklyn. (One of only two restaurants in Brooklyn to receive a Michelin star, too.)

Saul is the first to say he has had little to do with the café's daily operation. The public face and voice of the Food Company is its manager, Lynn Vinyard, who from

his first day on the job decided, "I was going to pretend that the front room of the café was the front room of my home, and anyone who came into it was going to have a good time."

The number of steady customers who patronize Boerum Hill daily—some of whom you could set your watch by—is substantial. At certain times of day, particularly in the morning after the 9 to 10:30 rush, there might not be anyone in the café who is not a regular. In fact, just at the point of describing this phenomenon, one Wednesday morning at 11, Lynn looked around the café and said, "I recognize every person here."

The regulars come directly from dropping their child off at Open House preschool around the corner. They come just after their morning tennis game at the New York Sports Club up the block. Teachers and parents alike come in droves from

PS 261 a few blocks away to have intense discussions about school dynamics and curriculum reform.

Others come with their laptops and stay for hours to work on their books or their funding proposals. Some come for meetings. Others come late in the afternoon—often for a second time that day, with their kids after school, to drink coffee and read the newspaper while their children drink hot chocolate and do their homework.

It is a diverse group of regular customers, most of whom are between the ages of thirty and fifty, older than the clientele at other cafés in the city. "I could turn the lights down, the music up, and change the menu to attract a younger crowd," says Lynn, "but then, where would this crowd go?

"This is not a cool Lower East Side place," adds Peter, one of the servers. "It's not too hip for its own good." Customers at Boerum Hill are down-to-earth—*hamish*, in Yiddish.

Even the Food Company's "celebrity" customers are of a different order than celebrity patrons elsewhere. Their names are more likely to be found in the *New York Times Book Review* than, say, on the *New York Post*'s tabloid inspired Page Six. Writers like Jonathan Letham (*Motherless Brooklyn* and *The Fortress of Solitude*), who grew up in the neighborhood and still lives here when not at his home in Maine. Or Jonathan Ames (*My Less Than Secret Life*). Or Michael Thomas (*Man Gone Down*). Or the children's book author and illustrator, Tad Hills (*Duck & Goose*) and artists such as Ivo Perelman, the avant-garde jazz musician and abstract painter.

Part of Lynn's genius, aside from showing customers a good time—such a good time, that between talking and laughing customers are known to forget to drink their coffee —is his ability to hire a staff of servers with extraordinary people skills. As Saul says, "These are not your average birds."

Unlike wait staff at most places who essentially serve customers and then let them be, here there is an inordinate amount of interaction between customer and staff. "In fact," says Lynn, "I have so much social interaction here that on my days off, I sit at home with the lights out and the TV off. Completely silent and dark."

"I remember the day after Bush was re-elected," says Sam, who has worked at Boerum Hill for years. "All the parents who came in were in shock. The air was really dense. People crying, nervous about the future. The place got very crowded. No one was moving. Everyone was just standing around, consoling one another. And as I looked out onto the room, at that moment, I realized how much our customers shared values and cared about the same things.

"I went around the room serving people coffee and whatever. I knew what everyone ordered, so I didn't have to ask. And as I did, I found myself hugging customers. Consoling them. The sense of community was amazing."

Asked to explain how the Food Company evolved to be a place with such a sharply defined sense of community, Sam replies, "I don't really know. I don't think anyone or

anything in particular is responsible. There is just something organic and very genuine about it. In other words, it was left to its own devices, and it just happened. And it continues to happen, in the way a forest after a fire regenerates itself and keeps growing and flourishing."

There is no doubt that ambiance and sense of community is what makes the Food Company the unique neighborhood place that it is, but its food and drink get high marks as well. The food menu is not extensive, but the ingredients are always fresh and the preparation careful. Much of the baking is done on the premises. (Soups, which are made at Saul, are particularly excellent.)

In the early years, Peet's Coffee in Seattle shipped to the Food Company on a weekly basis, but "At nine dollars a pound, what with free refills and all, we were losing money," laments Saul. For the past several years, the coffee has come from Gorilla Coffee, "The 101 percent Fair Trade, Brooklyn Roasted Shop" in nearby Park Slope. As the name "Gorilla" implies, the coffee is… well… strong.

For its brewed coffee, the Food Company uses a deep roasted Nicaraguan bean, which results in a full body coffee with a sweet and nutty flavor. It is not, according to Gorilla Coffee roasters, "for the weak of heart." The decaf is made from a Mexican bean grown high in the mountains of Chiapas.

Espresso is made from Gorilla's deep roast Brazilian coffee, which makes a rich espresso with a slight chocolaty taste. The Food Company uses an old, two-group, Italian made Michelangelo espresso maker. Or, as Lynn describes it, "A two-group, five-repair-bill-a-year espresso machine!"

Restaurant or coffeehouse? Maybe that is not the question. Will I get one of those window seats and how long will I stay? *That* is the question.

Short Cups

Boerum Hill and Cobble Hill, along with the other adjoining neighborhoods of Carroll Gardens to the south and Brooklyn Heights to the north, are the epitome of *neighborhood*, and thus, unsurprisingly, abound with intimate cafés with loyal followings. In Boerum Hill they include: **Flying Saucer Coffee & Tea Bar** (494 Atlantic Avenue between Nevins and Third), **The Nascent Café** (143 Nevins Street at Bergen), and **The Victory** (336 State Street at Hoyt). In Carroll Gardens: **The Fall Café** (307 Smith Street between Union and President). In Cobble Hill: **Tea Lounge** (254 Court Street at Kane), the newest location of the Park Slope Tea Lounges (see page 182). In Brooklyn Heights: **Tazza** (311 Henry Street between State and Atlantic). And if for no other reason than the unparalleled views of the water and the Statue of Liberty—**Fairway Café** (480-500 Van Brunt Street at the water's edge) in Red Hook. Hard to get to and not exactly a gathering place (except for Fairway food shoppers), but this café located outdoors (enter from coffee section of store), and enclosed in winter, offers a most extraordinary setting.

· 13 ·

PARK SLOPE

Family friendly, gay friendly, freelancer friendly, and young person friendly, the Slope's tree-lined streets of elegant and architecturally eclectic townhouses and brownstones can appear almost iridescent. With gas lamps along many of its sidewalks, some streets literally glow. Close to Manhattan and bordering on Prospect Park, the Slope extends from Flatbush Avenue to 15th Street, between the Park and Fourth Avenue. Along Seventh Avenue and, more recently, Fifth Avenue, Park Slope overflows with restaurants, bars, and cafés (a new café seems to open every week) making it a rarity among Brooklyn neighborhoods—one with a night life! And stand on any corner of any street in the Slope, cast a pebble over your shoulder, and you're likely to hit a writer, editor, or publisher.

Café Regular

**318A 11th Street (between
Fourth and Fifth Avenues)
(718) 768-4170
Open 7AM–8PM Mon to Sat
8AM–8PM Sun
Subway: F, M, R to 4th Avenue
& 9th Street**

Café Regular is an unpretentious café on an unpretentious block on the ground floor of an unpretentious brownstone. Yet, except for the coffee—regular and not decaf—there is nothing regular about it. In the way that a negative multiplied by a negative equals a positive, Café Regular proves regular times regular can equal distinctive.

For those who subscribe to the notion that small is beautiful, Café Regular is ideal. Consisting of 300 or so square feet (and that's if you include the bathroom), this café evokes the feel of a European neighborhood corner café. It is not for those who like to spread out nor for those wide of girth. Be prepared to sidle—sideways might be the only way to navigate the narrow space between the large, long wood and granite bar and the tables on the opposite wall.

The café's four tables are secured to the wall rather than the floor and give the appearance of desks of the sort one sees in elementary schools. "Yes, they do look like something out of study hall," admits Martin O'Connell, the Irish expat owner.

The small space dictates much of what transpires here. In addition to four tables that accommodate two persons each, there are two stools at the counter in the front.

Otherwise, one stands at the bar, as one does in European-style espresso bars, though a brass foot rail makes standing infinitely more comfortable than it would otherwise be. The ashtrays attached to the front of the bar are there, according to the always droll Martin, "For when the mayor repeals the no-smoking in public places law."

The fact that Café Regular cannot accommodate large numbers of customers at any one time seems not to be a shortcoming. "Actually," says Martin, "the smallness of the space was an attraction. It forces interaction. Larger places are more anonymous. Here it's as if you went into a little store in upstate New York, where upon entering you just naturally start talking to someone."

Steady customers echo this sentiment. One regular, a young Norwegian woman, explained, "Everything nowadays is so big. This is small and original. You don't see a lot of computers here. People come in for coffee, or to read. People are friendly here. They have this little *Cheers* thing going. When I first passed the sign above the café, I immediately said 'This is *my* café.' Just the smallness of the place and the coziness of the sign."

Martin left his native Limerick at age eighteen to work in hotels in England, although his last job in London was managing a coffee shop. Around the turn of the new millennium, at the urging of his sister who was living in Brooklyn, he came to New York. "I needed a change of scenery," he says.

"Our original idea was to open a café in the Fourth Avenue subway station. It would be like one of those stand-up espresso bars you see in all the train stations in Italy. With people coming and going, the Fourth Avenue station would have been ideal, but the MTA [Metropolitan Transit Authority] was not interested. So we found this place, just around the corner and up the street from the subway."

He claims his sister designed Café Regular, but, in truth, it looks more accumulated than designed. With pressed-tin walls and ceilings—painted a dark orange-red—the space is filled with a little of this and a little of that—an antique lamp, an old clock, some black-and-white family photos here and there (several of Martin's parents and one of him as a young "boulevardier" and don't let him fool you into believing it's his more handsome twin brother—there is none!). It works amazingly well (maybe it *was* by design?), and although the café opened in 2004, it looks like it has been in this spot forever. The black rotary phone (one of a handful left in New York City) on the wall behind the bar contributes to this sense of longevity.

Martin says he once saw a photograph in a magazine of a café in Italy that looked just like Café Regular. "Those bastards must have copied me."

Thinking about Italian cafés leads him to expound upon the preposterousness of Howard Schultz, the founder of Starbucks, being inspired to start his coffee empire by hanging out in cafés in Italy. To Martin, the similarity between a Starbucks and an Italian café—size wise, use-wise, and every otherwise—is non-existent. You will not, for example, find Italians in Rome sitting at their favorite espresso bar in Trastevere working on their laptops for four hours and not talking to a soul the entire time.

Martin, who lives next door and comes by to have his morning coffee even on his days off, runs Café Regular as if it were a neighborhood pub. He acts the bartender he imagines himself being rather than the barista he is, which makes perfect sense, since his parents owned a pub in Ireland, and Martin grew up within the Irish pub ethos. "A pub in Ireland is different than a café in New York," he says, "but in so far as social interaction is concerned, they both operate on the same principle."

Social engagement, which here often entails quick repartee and good-natured ribbing between Martin and his customers, is the sine quo non of Café Regular. "I don't make massive amounts of money," Martin says. "Social interaction is what makes it worthwhile."

And, as one customer—a German woman who claims to come here everyday even though she lives at the other end of the Slope—puts it, "Martin is fun."

Stay at Café Regular for an afternoon, and chances are not a single customer will be a first-timer. Given its location on a quiet residential block, there is not much foot traffic. It is more likely that customers from outside the immediate neighborhood will come by on weekends.

During the week, a steady stream of customers drifts in and out almost non-stop. Most all of the regular customers come within a four or five block radius of the café. "There is one woman," says Martin, "who comes with her laptop and stays for four or five hours—I have no idea what she does on it, but most run in for a cup of coffee, chat a little, go back to work or home, come back a couple of hours later for coffee and conversation, and so on. (There are two electrical outlets for computer use, and although there is no Wi-Fi access, you can steal a signal from across the street.)

"Some of our customers come two or even three times a day. It's very much a part of their daily routine. One couple comes literally every day, several times a day, for coffee. At 4:30 this afternoon, the guy of the couple will be back. It's like an addiction. They happen to be Jewish, and when I closed on Christmas, they actually complained!"

An inordinately large number of foreigners—many Europeans as well as Canadians, Australians, and, of course, the Irish—are regulars. It may have something to do with the café's European sensibility. Or the strong coffee they're used to.

The coffee is outstanding. "Better than anywhere else in the Slope, including those places that roast their own," says one Café Regular regular (sounds like the Major Major character from *Catch-22*) with conviction.

"The primary focus," says Martin, "is to serve good coffee," and the no-nonsense menu written on the mirror behind the bar attests to that. It reads, *in full*: Coffee, Tea, Espresso, Cappuccino, Latte, Hot chocolate, Iced tea or coffee, Fresh orange juice, Pastries, Egg."

"What we offer," Martin explains, "is basic and very minimal. If I owned a bar tomorrow, I would offer just two draft beers. If I had a restaurant, I would offer only two entrees, two appetizers and one dessert. I prefer to serve twenty people at a high level rather than two hundred for whom you're just slapping food out."

The coffee comes from the Philadelphia boutique roaster La Colombe Torrefaction, which is the coffee served in some of New York's most highly regarded restaurants such as Daniel and Le Bernardin. Martin characterizes La Colombe coffee as "strong but smooth"—"once you try it, you don't want any other."

For its brewed coffee, Café Regular uses the Corsica blend, a strong, dark roasted coffee with what the roaster describes as a "rounded taste." And for its espresso, Nizza is the five-bean blend coffee of choice. It is a medium roast, northern Italian-style coffee that makes a soft, delicate espresso with a slight caramel taste.

Espresso drinks are made on an Italian two-group La Spaziale machine. Martin makes his drinks with incredible care and meticulousness, which, of course, takes time, and cites the willingness of serious coffee drinkers to wait for their espresso or cappuccino. "In, say, Italy or France," he maintains, "people are willing to wait for their coffee. Their feeling is, if I'm going to be late for work, well, then I'll be late." Coffee comes first.

Martin had prior experience in London making latte art, although a La Colombe employee showed him some finer points when he arrived in New York. As good as he is—and he is very good—he admits to being not nearly as good as Josh George, one of his two part-time baristas (two part-time employees who together comprise one full-time person is all the help Martin employs), who honed his skills in a coffeehouse in Kansas City and is a latte artist extraordinaire.

There is an "international" selection of teas, "imported from distant places such as Ireland." Hot chocolate is made from French Valrhona chocolate. The orange juice is squeezed fresh. Pastries, such as croissants, come from the Brooklyn-based La Marquet Patisserie; walnut raisin rolls from the Sullivan Street Bakery in Manhattan; and hard-boiled eggs from Deli Beyond in Queens.

Although he attributes certain things to his sister (does he really even have a sister?) or his non-existent "more handsome twin brother," in fact, whatever Café Regular is or is not, Martin must take full credit—or blame, if your taste runs to cavernous, sofa-strewn, computer-dominated lounge spaces—for he *is* Café Regular. One could not exist without the other. Without Café Regular, Martin would be a man without purpose; a humorous, sardonic, ironic, and loquacious man without an outlet. Without Martin, Café Regular would be 300 square feet of space without a soul. And it would be oh so very quiet.

Try to come here and order a coffee, and not exchange a word with Martin. Well nigh impossible.

Tea Lounge

837 Union Street
(between 6th & 7th Avenues)
(718) 789-2762
www.tealoungeny.com
Open 7AM–1PM Mon to Thurs
7AM–2AM Fri; 8AM–2AM Sat
8AM–1PM Sun
Subway: 2, 3 to Grand Army Plaza

The Tea Lounge is not your cozy little neighborhood café. It is your cavernous 4,000-square-feet beehive of activity neighborhood café. "The Monstrosity on Union Street" some call it, referring to its size. It is a happening place, crowded and lively at almost any time of day. Walk into the Tea Lounge in the middle of the afternoon, and it is likely you'll encounter 50 people (doesn't anyone work a 9 to 5 job?) engaged in any number of activities (or inactivity, in the case of sleeping babies).

Some are reading. Others chatting. Many working on laptops. Someone may be playing one of the two coin-operated video games. Playing chess, or even cribbage. Groups meeting in one of the half-dozen dispersed seating clusters—support groups, parents groups, nanny groups. There are sing-alongs for children two mornings a week, live music (mostly jazz or jazz-inspired) Thursday and Friday evenings, movies on Monday nights, book readings and private parties of all sorts, including CD release parties, Kawali (traditional Indian and Pakistani Islamic music) parties, and bar and bat mitzvahs.

"This is a place for the whole community, not a slice of the community", says Greg Wolf, who co-owns the café with Jonathan Spiel. "That's what I'm most proud

of. That the Tea Lounge is for everyone; from babies to the elderly, every color, every ethnicity, every sexual orientation. It is 100 percent reflective of the neighborhood. And vice versa. Everyone finds their time of day to come."

Greg opened the original Tea Lounge in 2000 (on 7th Avenue at 10th Street; see page 182) and teamed up with Jonathan about six months later. The Union Street location opened in 2003 in what had previously been an environmentally-friendly laundromat.

"After my wife and I left Israel with our baby and moved back to Brooklyn," says Greg, "I realized that there was no place in this neighborhood to meet other babies. So, I was looking to open a place that would serve as a community hub for caregivers. A place that would serve the finest drinks."

In this respect, the Tea Lounge has certainly been successful. Parents, babies, toddlers—and strollers—are very much a part of the daily Tea Lounge landscape. "If you have no children, you tend to be less tolerant of kids being here," Greg maintains. "For those people, I suggest coming later in the day. [Late afternoon and early evening, there is not a baby in the house.] But we are one of the few places around where little kids can go up to the counter and order for themselves. And we actually train staff to handle kids. Kids grow up here. It's a beautiful thing."

"There are a lot of children in the neighborhood whose first words were 'Tea Lounge,'" adds Jonathan.

The vastness of space and large array of seating alternatives allow patrons who are there for different purposes to co-exist. Couches and easy chairs are grouped around coffee tables and also scattered here, there, and everywhere for more solitary sitting. There are straight-back chairs, a table with benches that looks like it could have come from a Dunkin' Donuts, several highchairs for toddlers, one large, extremely inviting "massage chair" ($1 for three minutes... $10 for a half hour!), stools at the alcoholic beverage bar and a long communal table with seating for a dozen people at the far end of the space.

When one looks out over the Tea Lounge, one quickly discerns discrete areas of quiet or noise; concentric circles of differing use. Around the perimeter of the café (the quietest and best lit areas), are the laptop users, silently—and, more often than not, singly—occupied. As one moves toward the center, toward the clusters of coffee table seating areas—the chatter grows louder. The Tea Lounge is not only about picking one's time of day to accommodate one's particular mood and purpose, but picking one's location inside.

The eclectically designed café incorporates motifs from the world's major tea cultures—the Middle East and Near East, North Africa and South Asia—including Punkah palm leaf ceiling fans, which operate in a strangely quiet way amidst the usual Tea Lounge hubbub.

During daytime hours the Tea Lounge is filled with students, caregivers and their charges, and many freelancers—with whom Park Slope abounds—who come with their computers and stay for hours. (The weekday evening crowd is younger and includes a date crowd. On weekends? Well, weekends are just crazy.) For some, Tea Lounge functions as an extension of their living room, people who Jonathan says

would "otherwise be cramped up in their small apartments."

For others, the Tea Lounge serves as their place of work. "Sometimes I feel I'm paying their rent," says Greg. "They come here to work; to run their businesses from here on their laptops. And they stay all day."

"Wireless can be a double-edged sword," adds Jonathan. "On the one hand, it brings in customers. At the same time, they stay longer. But, that's okay. We want customers to stay…We have comfortable seating here to encourage people to stay. Did you ever think about why McDonalds has uncomfortable chairs?"

While Greg had an extensive coffee background ("Ernesto Illy of Illy Coffee, whom I met in 1994 at a coffee convention in New Orleans, taught me everything."), having started and run three coffee bars in Haifa, Israel in the 1990s ("Israel has the best café culture in the world," he insists; "no other place is even close"), and whose family had a coffee roasting business in Maine; Jonathan, who came from the advertising world, had none. "Greg knew everything, and I knew nothing," Jonathan admits. "So, I worked shifts behind the bar for a year to learn what I needed to learn."

Despite its name, the Tea Lounge, sells far more coffee than tea. "We are a coffee country after all," says Jonathan. All of its coffee comes from Benbow's, in Bar Harbor, Maine, which was started by Greg's uncle and is, Greg says, "an eco, micro, 100 percent certified organic, Fair Trade, rainforest and bird-friendly roaster."

"We order the coffee one day, just out of the roaster, and it arrives at Tea Lounge the next morning. Fresh as can be."

The brewed coffees include: the Tea Lounge Blend, a medium roast combination of Ethiopian (Yirgacheffe) and Costa Rican (Doka) beans; Dark Sumatra (Takengon); Hazelnut (using organic flavoring); and Mexican Decaf (using a Swiss water decaffeination process).

For its espresso drinks, Tea Lounge uses a French/Italian roast that combines eight different kinds of beans. (It also uses a back-up espresso machine for making its signature "Eggspressos," which are scrambled eggs made with the steamer on the espresso machine.)

Besides the standard brewed coffee and espresso offerings, a Turkish Coffee with fresh cinnamon and cardamon, made from a blend of Greg's own invention, is served straight or as a latte or mocha. (Greg's idea of the Middle East meeting the West.) And, too, there is Tea Lounge's Shot Chocolate, which entails pouring espresso shots into hot chocolate. "The finest drink on the planet," intones Greg. "We have customers who have left intensive care units to get their Shot Chocolate!"

And, of course, there are teas. More than eighty! Which can be overwhelming for the uninitiated. "We offer more teas than most any other place," explains Jonathan, "because we want to give people the opportunity to discover something new."

There are black and green teas (including decaf), herbal teas, fruit blends, and chai. All are ordered by the pot and are served in a way that incorporates three of the major tea cultures in the world: an English teapot, on a Moroccan tea tray, with an Asian teacup. (One of the tea drinks, Yerba Mate, a traditional South American herbal tea, is served with a gourd!)

Taking their philosophy of providing something for everyone to its logical extension, in addition to the already mentioned coffees and teas, Tea Lounge offers a number of what they call their Proprietary Drinks—invented cocktails, many of which have coffee or tea added to them. There is wine and beer, including ten draft beers. And there is light fare.

And the music? According to Greg, it falls into one of four categories: The Grateful Dead ("they're my passion and I won't give them up"), jazz, local artists, and the baristas's choice, which one assumes could be anything.

Yep—something for everyone. And then some.

Note: There are two other Tea Lounge locations. The original is further south in Park Slope, at 350 7th Avenue (at 10th Street). Subway: F to 7th Avenue. And the newest Tea Lounge (opened in 2006) in nearby Cobble Hill at 254 Court Street (between Kane and Butler Streets). Subway: F, G to Bergen Street. Both these other locations are smaller than Union Street, and as such tend to be more intimate.

Union Street is the more dynamic, larger, more event-based café. Otherwise all three Tea Lounges share a common design, menu, hours of operation, and ethos; all cater to essentially the same Brooklyn demographic of young, or youngish, local residents, students, freelancers of all ages, caregivers, and children. All locations have their share of celebrity customers, which in Park Slope means, more likely than not, writers, it having perhaps the greatest concentration of writers per square block of any neighborhood in New York—or maybe anywhere, for that matter.

The 7th Avenue Tea Lounge, though only a ten-minute walk from its Union Street sibling, attracts a somewhat younger crowd, given that its more southerly location is somewhat less expensive than the north Slope neighborhood in and around Union Street. The other distinguishing feature of this one is the ghosts. "Out of the blue, a faucet will turn on by itself," claims Jonathan. "Or, an alarm will start beeping for no reason. An old alarm that was not supposed to work, and hadn't for who knows how long, all of a sudden went off. I ripped out the wires, and weeks later, it started beeping again.

"Another time, we lit candles in the café for the evening, and when it was time to close, I couldn't blow one of them out. I kept trying but couldn't. It reached the point where only the wick was left, and yet the flame kept burning; no matter how much or how hard I blew on it. Finally, I poured water on it, and as I did, the flame shot up the wall, raced across the ceiling and then, just as suddenly, disappeared. Just like that. Maybe there is a scientific explanation for it. But if there is, I have no idea what it could be. I believe it was a ghost."

You be the judge. And remember, by all accounts, it—or they—is friendly.

Short Cups

A new café opens in Park Slope seemingly every week. It's hard to keep track. Let's hope they won't close at the same rapid pace. In any event, among the many worthy neighborhood cafés in Park Slope are: **Cocoa Bar** (228 Seventh Avenue between 3rd and 4th), **Café Eleven** (381 Seventh Avenue between 11th and 12th), Lonelyville (154 Prospect Park West between Vanderbilt and Seeley), **Ozzie's Coffee & Tea** (57 Seventh Avenue at Lincoln and 251 Fifth Avenue between Carroll and Garfield), and **Red Horse Café** (497 Sixth Avenue at 12th). And on the lower edges of Park Slope, where Park Slope meets Gowanus, is the **Mule Café** (67 Fourth Avenue between Bergen and St. Mark's). With its on-premises micro-coffee roaster and long communal table out back—large enough to seat half the population of Brooklyn—it is the perfect neighborhood café. In nearby Windsor Terrace is **Crossroads Café** (1421 Prospect Avenue at Reeve). And on the Prospect Heights side of Flatbush Avenue is the **Heights Coffee Lounge** (335 Flatbush Avenue between Park and Seventh).

GREENPOINT/WILLIAMSBURG

The north Brooklyn neighborhoods of Greenpoint and Williamsburg are ethnically diverse, mostly middle- and working-class areas, that have, despite much industrial and light manufacturing and a less-than-elegant housing stock, in recent years become magnets for young people priced out of Manhattan. Williamsburg, around Bedford Avenue on the north side, is a thriving, hip, cultural, culinary, and shopping destination. Williamsburg was the first to receive this wave of new gentry. Greenpoint followed. Bushwick can't be far behind as "urban pioneers" continue to move further east. Recent arrivals live side by side with the older and well established ethnic communities of mostly European origin. Greenpoint—sometimes referred to as "Little Poland"—is the second largest Polish enclave in the United States.

Gimme! Coffee

**495 Lorimer Street
(between Powers and Grand Streets)
(718) 388-7771
www.gimmecoffee.com
Open 7AM–8PM daily
Subway: L to Lorimer;
G to Metropolitan Ave**

*W*hen the owner of the small Ithaca-based Gimme Coffee chain of espresso bars decided to open a coffeehouse in New York City, it was no accident that Williamsburg was the neighborhood of choice. A newly arrived young, artsy population, inexpensive rents, and the fact that Gimme's master coffee roaster's daughter lived in the neighborhood aligned the stars toward this part of Williamsburg, east of the Brooklyn Queens Expressway and bordering on Bushwick.

Gimme, as it is familiarly known, opened in December of 2003, and by 2005 the minimally designed and decorated, coffee-driven café had been selected as "Best NYC Coffeehouse" by AOL City Guide and Citysearch. And in September of 2006 came the *coup de grace*. A long article about espresso in the *New York Times* included Gimme among the best artisanal coffee shops in the city. Following that, it was featured in a Martha Stewart TV program about New York City espresso bars.

"When we first opened, business was slow," says Mike White, who has managed Gimme's Brooklyn location since its inception. "In fact, for several weeks, I stood out

on the street and passed out flyers… It wasn't until the *Times* article that business really took off. Our business increased 60 percent the first weekend after the article appeared, and it has been increasing ever since. During the week we still get the locals, but since the article, on weekends we now get people from out of the neighborhood, out of the city, out of state, out of the country—we call them the 'Weekend Warriors'—and lines are often out the door. From the original staff of three, we now have a staff of ten."

Mike White, born and raised in Ithaca (though he's quick to point out that his father was born in Brooklyn)—is the public face of Gimme. Mike met Kevin Cuddeback, the founder of the Gimme "chain" (if four locations, a trailer, and a stall doth a chain make) during Mike's young adult perambulations.

"A mutual friend told me Kevin said he would never hire me," Mike recalls. "I think he thought I wasn't manageable. But then I started working for him in Ithaca… and when a couple of people he had in mind to manage the Brooklyn location didn't work out, I guess he was desperate. So he hired me. The good thing about it is Ithaca doesn't really know what we're doing here!"

"When I first started working for Kevin, I knew nothing about coffee. I was a blank slate. But Gimme's environment was conducive to learning and experimentation. And I'm still learning. I still work the bar, because it's the only way to gauge the energy of the place and its needs.

"Recently I took a trip 'to origin' in Mexico, since we get a lot of our coffee from there. It was absolutely life-changing to see where it all comes from… It's equally intense on that side—the growing side—as it is on the roasting and brewing side. In the future, I would love to work to improve the conditions for growing coffee in an ecologically sustainable way."

At Gimme, anything that does not contribute directly to the making of coffee detracts from it. For that reason, no food (other than pastries, provided daily by Balthazar in Manhattan) is offered. "Coffee demands one hundred percent attention to do it well," says Mike. "The more time we spent on other items would mean less time spent on coffee. We don't, for example, sell bagels. It would take time to toast them. Time to put on a spread. We would never have an oven or a stove. I am considering adding some savories—quiches—but we wouldn't heat them. Customers would buy them and heat them at home or at work."

For its espresso drinks (many of which are given seemingly improbable names such as "Crazy Fiona," "Mad Cupid," "Mocha Mint Phatty") Gimme uses its medium-dark Leftist Northern Italian espresso blend, a proprietary blend (Mike won't reveal the beans other than an Ethiopian Harar) that yields a rich shot with a "chocolate and tobacco aftertaste."

As Mike explains, "The blend is constantly evolving, depending on the harvests, the weather, everything that affects the coffee bean. If the particular Harar we use in the Leftist blend is different from before, it has to be balanced differently. And then each type of bean is chosen to complement the others."

Although Gimme Brooklyn started with a much talked about and highly praised custom-made two-group, Dutch-made Mirage espresso machine, it has since been replaced it with a larger, three-group La Marzocca. (And by the way, Gimme pulls all their espressos as *triple* ristrettos.) "It was used in the 2006 United States Barista Championships held in Charlotte, North Carolina," says Mike. "We bought it right off the floor. It's a competition grade machine. It's bigger than the Mirage. Not only three-group as opposed to two, but it has a larger boiler; actually two of them, one just for steaming milk. But the best feature is the temperature control. Adjustable to one-tenth of a degree."

All espresso based drinks—even the macchiatos—are topped with lovely latte art. And lest anyone doubt the seriousness and attention to detail that Gimme requires of all its baristas, a 120-page "Barista Manual" has been prepared for their use and constant reference.

For its brewed coffee, Gimme Brooklyn offers—on a rotating basis—the twenty or so varietals roasted by Gimme Coffee in Ithaca and shipped to Brooklyn twice a week. These include coffees from all the major coffee growing regions of the world, among them: Bolivia, Brazil, Colombia, Ethiopia, Guatemala, India, Java, Kenya, Mexico, Rwanda, and Sumatra.

Gimme also sells these coffees by the pound. Deep Disco, a medium-dark roast Mexican blend, is matched in popularity by three espresso blends: Leftist, French Roast (a darker Southern Italian roast compared to the milder Leftist Northern Italian roast), and Platinum Blonde (a medium roast, four-bean blend).

If in perusing the menu, with its three major sections—Espresso, Brewed Coffee, Not Coffee—you wonder what "BYOTM −.15" means, it is "Bring Your Own Travel Mug" and take fifteen cents off the price of your drink. "Okay, maybe that's a little obsessive," admits one of the baristas sheepishly.

No one comes to Gimme Coffee for its decor or its roominess. They come for the excellent coffee. (Mike estimates they sell *maybe* twenty cups of tea a day.) Longer than it is wide, Gimme, formerly a drum shop, is a relatively small space with a handful of tables and a few additional chairs strategically placed so no one will trip over the feet of those sitting in them, though this doesn't always work during the morning rush. A couple of stools on the other side of the bar are referred to as the V.I.P. chairs, for regulars who know of their existence and use them to talk to the baristas.

Despite certain challenges of space, Gimme's energy makes it a welcoming place with a huge coterie of regulars. Monday through Friday it is patronized almost exclusively by locals, who Mike admits are the more recently arrived young people as opposed to the old-time Italian, Polish, and Hispanic residents. "The real old-timers have a hard time justifying the expense," he says. "But if they don't come in, their children do, or will." Mike points to a guy talking to a group of young women. "He lived with his mother and never came in when she was alive. But once she died, he began coming in. Now he comes everyday and always starts conversations. He talks up strangers. It's hard to imagine what he would do without Gimme Coffee."

There is a weekday morning rush of suits and ties, followed by a second wave of local artists, writers, designers, actors, musicians, producers, and students who come in and often stay. Freelancers abound in this part of Brooklyn, and Gimme Coffee often serves as job central. "People get jobs from each other," says Mike. "Customers even hire our baristas for freelance jobs."

As in most cafés these days, laptop use is prevalent at Gimme, but one wouldn't say it is prevails. The café doesn't exactly discourage its use, but Mike would rather see people talking. There were a couple of outlets when Gimme took over the space, but they did not add outlets. Nor have they added free wireless access, though Mike admits a signal from the neighborhood can easily be stolen.

Scanning the café, Mike looks to see which of the patrons he knows: everyone except one couple. And he and his staff know their drinks, too—"eighty percent of the drinks of our Monday through Friday customers."

After some reflection, adds, "Actually, it's pretty easy to do, since people always order the same drink. People are so regular."

Café Grumpy

**193 Meserole Avenue
(at Diamond Street)
(718) 349-7623
www.cafegrumpy.com
Open 7AM–7PM Mon to Fri
9AM 7PM Sat
9AM–6PM Sun
Subway: G to Nassau or Greenpoint**

Almost from its inception, the decidedly "coffee-centric" Café Grumpy has been known to those who track cafés serving excellent coffee and espresso. Grumpy opened in November 2005, and just four months later it was already included in a *Daily News* article listing seven of the city's most exceptional cafés—exceptional for the quality of their coffee.

Located in the heavily Polish section of Greenpoint, where homes with aluminum siding meet red brick warehouses (a palpable reminder that parts of Brooklyn can still flex their manufacturing muscle), Café Grumpy, formerly a bar, is a welcome addition to this neighborhood east of McGuiness Avenue where there are few stores and services. It's a welcome alternative to the "very sweet" coffee of the Polish bakeries along the Manhattan Avenue–Greenpoint hub.

No one could have predicted that husband and wife Caroline Timbrell and Chris Bell would one day own a café whose reputation rests primarily on the high quality of its coffee, for neither knew much about coffee.

"I started drinking coffee before high school," Caroline says. "But it was always diner coffee. And then all through high school [in suburban New Jersey] we would go to a diner to hang out. We drank coffee, but the coffee was incidental. It was the excuse to stay and talk with friends. It didn't matter what it tasted like."

Chris, on the other hand, grew up in a small New South Wales town in Australia, a country with a well-developed café tradition. "There were loads of European immigrants who settled in Australia, so they brought their European café culture with them," he says.

Their education about coffee began in earnest after they met while working in the same midtown Manhattan bank. They would go out together for coffee, and, as they developed their coffee palates, came to realize there were relatively few places that sold a really terrific cup of coffee. Fewer still were the cafés that not only served good coffee but were also comfortable and enjoyable places in which to spend time.

The more cafés they went to, the more they thought about starting their own. At a certain point, they decided they had talked long enough. It was time to take the risk. Chris scrapped plans to return to Australia. They spent a year scoping out other cafés around the city, taking notes. (And getting married.)

"Ultimately," says Chris, "there were two major things I disliked and would make sure we avoided in our café: Bad or stale coffee. And attitude—servers who acted as if they were doing you a favor. In fact, at one particular café, the waitress gave us such a hard time that when we left, I said this place should have been called 'Café Grumpy.' And that's how we got our name."

"Once we said it," adds Caroline, "we saw the humor in it and decided to keep it. Most people think the name is funny, although a few have said it's negative. Some think it refers to how people feel in the morning before they have their coffee. People interpret the name and our logo, which my brother created, however they want.

"The name works. People relate to it. And," she adds with a wink, "we can use it as an excuse when we're not at our best. We all have bad days."

Café Grumpy occupies the entire ground floor of a three-story apartment building (originally the back part was gallery/performance space, but the wall was knocked down and the café expanded into it). In Manhattan, it would be almost prohibitively expensive to have a café of this size. It is no surprise, nor accident, that the Café Grumpy location in Chelsea (see page 200) is only a quarter of the size of this location. And if not four times the Greenpoint rent, certainly some multiple of it.

The space is bright and airy and roomy, with three distinct areas that together provide ample space for small tables and a large communal table with wrap-around bench, high tables with stools, and couches. The wood floors are new and polished. There are exposed brick walls, pressed tin ceilings painted white, and walls painted either white or bright orange. Though this may remind one of Creamsicles, the orange and white color combination is quite attractive and calming; it works remarkably well.

Large mirrors add a feeling of spaciousness to rooms that would feel spacious without them. In short, Café Grumpy's roominess—and the comfort that accompanies large spaces—is a luxury only such a relatively—and we do mean "relatively"—low-rent neighborhood can make possible.

From the beginning, high-quality coffee and espresso were to be paramount, and everything else would follow. Chris and Caroline went out to Victrola Coffee in Seattle for barista training. They read books and practiced, practiced, practiced. "At the beginning, Chris and I worked the bar seven days a week," says Caroline. "That's when the two of us could do latte art well."

Both Chris and Caroline readily admit that most all of their baristas do latte art better than they do, now that they've mostly given up their daily stint at the espresso machine. "And," they add almost in unison, "we have one guy, Peter, who is so good at latte art that we all call him 'the showoff.'"

Peter, who is from Tacoma, Washington and attributes his steamed milk making and pouring abilities to a string of café jobs in that area ("They were my escape route from making sandwiches at Quiznos,"), proceeds to make a latte topped with three delicate rosetta leaves. "I probably could have made four if the cup was bigger," says the showoff.

The coffee offerings are no-nonsense. Or, in the words of Tasha, a Grumpy barista, "There are no fluff drinks. Nothing like a 'frappaccino.' And the Chelsea store is even more about straight-up coffee drinks."

The "no fluff" coffee menu includes espresso-based drinks (Espresso, Americano, Macchiato, Cappuccino, Latte, and Mocha) and single-variety brewed coffees.

Triple ristretto espressos are pulled on a two-group Synesso Cyncra espresso machine and are made from Northern Italian Reserve from Ecco Caffe, a small boutique roaster in Santa Rosa, California. (Ecco roasts 500 to 600 pounds of beans a week compared to, 4,000 or more pounds typically roasted by a medium-sized company.) The Ecco Reserve is a blend of two Brazilian beans, relatively lightly roasted, giving the resulting espresso a "bitter-sweet chocolate, honey, almond and caramel finish."

The brewed coffees come from Counter Culture Coffee, the renowned, environmentally conscious roaster in Durham, North Carolina. Café Grumpy offers about a half dozen of their single origin coffees, prepared either by the French press method, in which case all are offered daily, or brewed by the pot, in which case only one or two are offered on any given day. These generally include coffees from Bolivia, East Timor, Kenya, El Salvador and Nicaragua.

And there are teas! A surprisingly large variety (and a surprisingly large percentage of Grumpy's business), given its coffee-centered reputation. Black, white, green, oolongs and fusions, all provided by the Art of Tea in Los Angeles, a purveyor of "hand-crafted batches." Tea classes at Café Grumpy, given by the Art of Tea, are in the offing.

That Café Grumpy has been embraced by the neighborhood is not surprising. Until quite recently, there were no other cafés like it in the immediate environs. Locals would have to go to neighboring Williamsburg or into Manhattan—parts of the city recent arrivals to Greenpoint had been priced out of and most likely the reason they landed in Greenpoint to begin with—to find anything that even approached it in quality of coffee and environment.

Although the primary customers are local residents, many who stay with their laptops for hours, Grumpy's reputation has made it a destination for people living outside the neighborhood—or, even, outside of the city. "We get lots of writers who come with their laptops," says Caroline. "But we also get coffee geeks from New Jersey!"

One of their most beloved regular customers is someone Chris and Caroline refer to as the "Decaf Guy." "We had been open just a day or two, and this guy comes in and orders a decaf coffee," Chris explains. "No one had ordered one before, and quite honestly, we weren't prepared. So, it took a while. But he waited around. He has been back literally every day since to get his decaf."

During the week and during the day, workers from nearby businesses make good use of this coffee oasis in their midst. Broadway Stages, the mammoth studio and sound stage facility located just across the street, has been known to submit orders for, say, "Coffee for 75," when a big feature film is being shot.

A clothes rack purchased from a sale after the shooting of *The Good Shepherd* (neither Robert DeNiro nor Matt Damon ever came into the café, but undoubtedly did drink its coffee) stands next to the restroom, a constant reminder of Hollywood's periodic and fleeting incursions into Brooklyn.

Chris and Caroline exude obvious pride in what they've created. "We were the first café in New York to have a Synesso. The first to use Counter Culture Coffee. The first to use a Clover [see note]. Our top baristas are actually salaried." Another first might be the highchairs—babies are not usually afforded high priority at coffeehouses.

"I look at the place when it's full," says Caroline, "and ask myself, 'Why are there all these people here?' And that's when I realize we've really built something."

Note: On November 15, 2006, one year to the day after opening Café Grumpy in Greenpoint, a second Café Grumpy opened in Manhattan, in Chelsea, at 224 W. 20th Street (between 7th and 8th Avenues). Subway: 1 to 23rd Street (7th Avenue) or C E to 23rd Street (8th Avenue). Substantially smaller than the Greenpoint location, it can never be quite the hanging-out place that defines its Brooklyn counterpart. And Chelsea, by design, has neither electrical outlets nor Wi-Fi.

Their motivation for opening the Chelsea location was twofold. "One, was to correct the mistakes we made," Chris begins. "Two places cannot be micro-managed. It forces us to look at the bigger picture. And secondly, we wanted to take coffee in a new direction. At Chelsea we present coffee as if it were a wine bar... we offer a wider variety there. Since we make each cup fresh and brewed to order, customers can try several kinds and come to know the nuances of each."

What makes this all possible is the Clover coffee machine, which did not exist until around March of 2006. Using a technology that combines two methods for making coffee, the French press and vacuum brewing, the Clover can make an individual cup of coffee, from beans freshly grounded just for that cup, in about forty seconds. Café Grumpy in Chelsea has two Clovers.

"So far," says Chris, "having two locations is more than twice the work. We spend our days on the subway shuttling back and forth between the two. I cannot wait for the time to come when I can spend a few hours drinking coffee and reading the newspaper in my own café."

Short Cups

Exit the L Train at the Bedford Avenue Station, and you are in the heart of the busiest thoroughfare in Williamsburg. It teems with people and places to eat and drink. Cafés extend onto the sidewalk, so you'll have no trouble finding them. Among the somewhat less obvious places—including those off the Bedford Avenue beaten path—are: **Atlas Café** (116 Havemeyer Street at Grand); **Fix Café** (110 Bedford Avenue at North 11th), newly renovated, which is entered either through Sound Fix (among the many neighborhood music stores selling new and used CDs as well as vinyl) or its own entrance on North 11th; **Café 1980** (150 Wythe Avenue at North 8th), which in addition to its excellent coffee, pastry, and foods makes its own peanut butter! (It's often referred to as St. Helen Café 1980 was the year Mt. St. Helen's erupted); **Oslo Coffee Company** (133-B Roebling Street at North 4th and 328 Bedford Avenue between South 2nd and 3rd); **Read Café** (158 Bedford Avenue between North 8th and 9th); and the **Roebling Tea Room** (143 Roebling Street at Metropolitan), particularly inviting as a hanging out place during off eating hours. In Greenpoint, there is **Eat Coffee Records** (124 Meserole Avenue between Eckford and Leonard), yet another vinyl record and CDs emporium cum café and the **Greenpoint Coffee House** (195 Franklin Street at Green), best experienced as a coffeehouse rather than a restaurant at off-dining hours. And just recently, a string of wonderful cafés have opened along the northernmost, less pedestrian dense strip of Manhattan Avenue. They include **Cafecito** (1015 Manhattan Avenue between Huron and Green), where besides their excellent coffee they have the coolest bathroom sink you'll find anywhere; **Champion Coffee** (1108 Manhattan Avenue between Dupont and Clay); and **Ashbox Café** (1154 Manhattan Avenue between Ash and Box).

· 15 ·

LONG ISLAND CITY

Located one subway stop from midtown Manhattan, Long Island City has long been a major warehousing-manufacturing-industrial area, adding some brawn to a city better known for its beauty and brains. The Citibank Tower looms above this otherwise low-rise neighborhood, and seems lonely and forlorn without companions of comparable size. The several high-rise, luxury apartment towers built along the waterfront, provide some kinship of scale, though a bit distant. If these new towers are ever fully occupied, the neighborhood's population of young professionals will increase dramatically. The Museum of Modern Art's temporary home in Long Island City during its major renovation (2002 to 2004) brought thousands to the area for the first time. MoMa QNS attracted up to 2,000 visitors a day— and even 4,000 a day during the Matisse–Picasso exhibit.

Communitea

**47–02 Vernon Boulevard
(at 47th Avenue)
(718) 729-7708
www.communitea.net
Open 7AM–8PM Mon to Fri
9AM–6PM Sat & Sun
Subway: 7 to Vernon
Blvd / Jackson Ave; G to
21st Street**

Although the name of Kafia Saxe, co-owner of Communitea, may suggest an affinity toward coffee (pronounced *ka fee' yeh*, and said to be part Hebrew, part Indian, and part Arabic), it was actually tea that was the impetus for her café. That, and the New York City marathon.

Kafia entered the 2002 marathon and met Communitea co-owner Lloyd Canning on their way to the race. They talked. Met up after they'd finished the 26.2 miles. Lloyd, an Irishman from County Clare, had immigrated to the United States to escape Ireland's economic doldrums. He was in the process of starting a bar in Long Island City. Kafia offered to lend a hand, Lloyd accepted the offer, and soon they were a couple.

Three years later, Lloyd's landlord offered him a space a couple of doors down from the bar for another business of his and Kafia's choosing. They thought that the largely industrial neighborhood, just a stone's throw from Manhattan and fast becoming more residential, could use a café. As an Irishman literally steeped in the tea tradition, Lloyd naturally thought teahouse rather than coffeehouse. Kafia was likewise partial to tea.

They traveled to North Carolina, where Kafia had grown up and gone to college, to check out a well-known teashop in Charlotte and were smitten. They didn't know how tea would be received in their gritty Queens neighborhood, but the new construction and conversion of commercial buildings to residential use promised a new influx of condo owners. They decided to take the risk. Take tea and see.

Shortly after leaving her job with a non-profit devoted to creating housing for low- and middle-income renters, a friend gave Kafia *Celebrating the Third Place: Inspiring Stories About the "Great Good Places" at the Heart of Our Communities*, by Ray Oldenburg. The "third place" refers to those public places where people can interact in a way they can't or don't at home (the first place) or at work (the second place)… "That's it," I said. "That's my goal. To create a café that would be that third place.

"I wanted the design to have a clean look, but at the same time relate aesthetically to the neighborhood. So we exposed the brick and kept the tin ceiling. We uncovered those wonderful columns in front when we demolished the original façade... We replaced the entire front with glass. It was far and away our single biggest expense. Two of those glass panels slide open, which creates a corner that is fully open. That was the brainchild of our architect. On nice days, everyone wants to sit in the corner." (The café happens to look out onto the route of the NYC Marathon, an annual reminder to Kafia and Lloyd of their first meeting.)

The glass facade brings in delicious light, and when opened, fresh air—the feeling is similar to being in a convertible with the top down—but what makes the facade truly special are the two large images painted on it. They're impossible to miss and almost as impossible to decipher.

"It's a long story," Kafia begins. "One morning a couple months after we opened, as I approached the café, I thought, 'Oh, no. We've been tagged.' Someone had written

'Rambo' and 'Ratsue' on the front glass. I tried to clean it, but… it had been etched on with acid. Within an hour, ten to fifteen people stopped to suggest how to get rid of it. Alcohol wipes. Razor blades. People coming with condolences and solutions. People really cared. *Their* café had been vandalized.

"Finally, an artist, one of the bartenders at Lloyd's bar, decided to cover it up… Using blue and black acrylic paints, she painted over the graffiti, which was hard, because the acid had dripped, leaving long marks. The finished work looks like something floral. Art nouveau. Almost like a tattoo. So, it turned out not to be the worst thing that could happen. It even gives us a little privacy. People think the painting on the window is intentional—until they read the note posted on the window. I tell people we made lemonade out of lemons. Originally I was going to say tea out of tea leaves or something, but that didn't sound quite right. So, yes, we made lemonade out of lemons… No laments. Keep moving forward."

Besides the glass facade (wear sunglasses if you're sitting up front on a bright, sunny day!), among the more distinctive features of this sleek, minimalist fifteen-table café is a bench for

table seating that extends almost the entire length of the space. The menu is written on the chalkboard wall at the café's far end, where toddlers draw, too.

While this is officially a teahouse that happens to also serve coffee, Kafia admits that during its first year or two, Communitea sold substantially more coffee than tea. "Certainly during the morning rush," she explains. "But, then, we would make up for it with tea in the afternoon. Now, we are getting to 50/50."

The coffee comes from Irving Farm Coffee Company (see page 88), in Millerton, New York. "Irving Farm taught us everything about coffee," says Kafia. "They set up our entire coffee program. What coffees to use. How to make them. They also got us our espresso machine (an old two-group, Italian Rancilio) and grinder. I just love that espresso machine. I love the red. I love the metal plates on the front. The curves. It reminds me of a car from the 1950s. I just love everything about it."

Her parting comment on the subject of coffee? "We are the only place in Queens that sells a good cup of coffee (10 oz.) for a dollar. Period."

Kafia, inveterate tea drinker that she is, brightens considerably when discussing tea. Her enthusiasm is obvious. "We get all our teas from one person. I won't tell you her name. I'll just say, she is based in Tarrytown, she's Indian and her family owns tea estates in India.

"We sell only loose leaf teas. No tea bags! And we infuse each order. We don't make gallons at a time. We make tea per cup or teapot. Blacks, greens, oolongs, whites, herbals. Teas from India, China, Japan, South Africa, Sri Lanka, Taiwan.

"All teas come from the same plant. (Herbal 'teas' not really being tea.) Tea is as complex as wine and affected by the same variables. The altitude. Weather. Amount of rainfall. The difference in teas is mostly about the difference in the amount of oxidation."

Kafia is especially devoted to the Lapsang Souchong from Fujian Province, China. It is smoked over a pinewood fire and, as she describes it, "It has the aroma of a burnt forest."

Perhaps the most popular tea is the Communitea English Breakfast, the house blend of Assam and Ceylon teas with a touch of Darjeeling.

In addition to the major tea groups, each group offers the option of flavored teas, typically flavored with fruits such as black currants, blueberries, coconut, melon, and peach or with ginger or vanilla. And if the tea menu at first glance seems overwhelming, don't despair. Rather, order the Grand Earl Gray, a Keemum tea from China flavored with bergamot oil, a natural antidepressant. Despair no more!

Customers are a mix of neighborhood residents and people who work nearby. "I would say the age range is 23 to 50," Kafia estimates. Regular customers include old-time and newly arrived locals, many of whom are freelancers, grad students, and people who do non-traditional jobs. Many artists and set designers who live and work in the studios that punctuate this area of Queens (not far, from P.S. 1 Contemporary Art Center, a museum affiliate of MoMA) drop by throughout the day.

And, of course, during lunch hour, there is an influx of office and construction workers. At least a half-dozen massive high-rise apartment buildings have been recently completed or are now in construction within a few block radius of Communitea. A board of education building is down the street. A blood bank office is coming to the neighborhood, and, when the weather is nice, workers from the Citibank building make the trek for lunch. Communitea offers an array of "comfort food" that includes sandwiches (including vegan hot dogs), soups, salads (accompanied by Communitea's own dressings) and panini. "We have a convection oven but no range," says Kafia. "We make whatever is feasible ourselves. I think we do a pretty damn good job with what we have. And, we offer the only pimento cheese sandwich to be found in Queens!"

Has she succeeded in creating a café that functions as the third place of her original fantasy? Without a moment's hesitation Kafia says, "I think so… My customers tell me I have… When their families visit, they bring them here and say, 'This is where I get my coffee.' People who move out of the neighborhood come back to visit. I have customers who offer to help when we're busy. People who come in for coffee on their way to work, come back for lunch. Then they come back later in the afternoon for more coffee. I see most of my regular customers twice a day.

"I'm proud of this place," she concludes. "It's my first baby. This is my second," she says, patting her belly.

In the future, expect to see a baby behind Communitea's counter.

Short Cups

Once the new apartment towers are filled, the added residential population of Long Island City, near the waterfront, should reach critical mass and encourage the opening of new cafés. Now, there is **Brasil Coffee House** (48–19 Vernon Boulevard), just up the block from Communitea. And, if one feels adventurous, the nearby Astoria section of Long Island City has many European-style Greek coffeehouses—on and off Broadway, which are patronized by what is said to be the largest concentration of Greeks outside Greece.

Coffee Glossary

American Roast—A light roast. Darker than what is referred to as a cinnamon roast, which is very light brown in color and highly acidic, but lighter than a City roast, which is at the upper end of the light roasts. An American roast is considered too light for espresso.

Americano—Though it looks like a cup of American brewed coffee, it is made with a single or double shot of espresso, to which six to eight ounces of hot water from the espresso machine is added. Since it's made to order, it is fresher, smoother and hotter than a cup of brewed coffee.

Arabica—Coffee beans that come from the species of coffee tree called *coffea arabica*, one of the two major categories of coffee trees (the other is *coffea canephora*, from which the robusta bean comes). Arabica beans are grown at higher elevations (3,000 to 6,000 feet) than robusta beans, develop more slowly, and as a result, are considered to be of a higher quality and more flavorful. They also have less caffeine than robusta beans.

Artisanal Coffee Movement—This movement is focused on—some might say obsessed with—the quality of coffee, beginning with the source of the bean and continuing through roasting, dosing, tamping, and extracting, and ending, maybe, with a little latte art on top.

Barista—An Italian term for those who make and serve espresso and espresso drinks. A 2002 article in the *New York Times* noted that being a barista in Italy was a profession, almost an art, while here it's considered a lousy job. Much has changed since then, thanks to the West Coast artisanal coffee movement, which has moved east.

Breve—An espresso drink with half-and-half, instead of milk.

Café au Lait—Equal parts brewed coffee (often a French roast) and steamed milk.

Caffe Mocha—Espresso, chocolate syrup (or powdered chocolate), and steamed milk, often topped with whipped cream. A venti (20 oz.) Caffe Mocha with whipped cream at Starbucks is said to contain 490 calories, the equivalent of a McDonald's Quarter Pounder with cheese.

Cappuccino—One-third espresso, one-third steamed milk, and one-third froth. A cappuccino with froth only is often referred to as a dry cappuccino. The name comes from Capuchin friars—some say the Capuchins invented the drink, others that the color of the coffee matched the color of their robes, and still others that their hoods (*cappuccios*) make a ring of brown around their faces, much like a cappuccino with its white milk/foam center surrounded by a brown rim of espresso.

City Roast—A light roasted coffee, roasted to a medium brown color, darker than an American roast, but lighter than a Full City roast, which begins the medium-roast range of coffees.

Clover—A newly invented coffee-maker designed to make single-cup, made-to-order brewed coffee. Using a technology that combines the French press and vacuum brewing, a single cup of coffee, for which the beans have been freshly ground, is made in forty seconds. At $11,000 a pop, don't expect to find the Clover at your neighborhood deli.

Corretto—Espresso with a shot of a liqueur such as cognac, brandy, or grappa.

Crema—A reddish-brown foam produced by the emulsified oils forced out of the coffee under the high pressure of the espresso making process. Proving that oil and water do indeed not mix, the crema sits atop the surface of the espresso, helping to seal in its flavors.

Cupping—The tasting of coffee, usually done after roasting to determine the right roast and blend. Hot water is poured over grounds to make a small sample for cupping purposes. Not unlike wine tasting—minus the spitting.

Doppio—A double shot of espresso: twice as much coffee is put in the portafilter, resulting in a two-ounce espresso.

Dosing—Creating (by grinding) and delivering (to portafilter) the correct amount of coffee for making espresso. About seven grams of finely ground coffee for a single shot, though many of the best artisanal coffeehouses use slightly more for added strength and flavor.

Espresso—A drink made by forcing hot water under high pressure over finely ground coffee. Although the defining feature of an espresso is the method used (water at nearly 200° Fahrenheit under about 135 pounds per square inch of pressure forced over 6–9 grams of finely ground compressed coffee for 22 to 25 seconds—plus or minus a couple—for a single, 1–1¼-oz. drink), the word "espresso" is also used to describe the blend of beans used to make the drink ("Espresso Blend") or any of the darker roasts that characterize the beans used to make it ("Espresso Roast").

Espresso Con Panna—An espresso topped with a dollop of whipped cream.

Estate Coffee—Typically meant to refer to coffee that comes from a single farm, though it might also be used to describe coffee produced by a single *group* of farms or a single mill. Usually the name of a coffee's estate, and, often, the proprietor's name as well, are identified, as in estate-produced wines.

Extraction—The drawing out of flavors from the coffee that results from the espresso making process. Over-extraction (done too slowly or with water too hot) results in bitterness. Under-extraction (done too quickly or with water not warm enough) results in a weak espresso.

Fair Trade—Coffee bought directly from farmer cooperatives, at a fair, guaranteed minimum price not subject to the vagaries of the market. Farmers from whom Fair Trade coffee is bought, typically produce their coffee under environmentally sound, sustainable conditions. Although fair traded coffee is not always organic, it usually is. To be certified Fair Trade in the United States, a producer must meet labor and trade practices established by TransFair USA.

French Press—A plunger pot method of brewing coffee. Hot water is added to coarse coffee grounds, stirred and left to steep for about four minutes. A nylon or stainless steel mesh plunger is then pushed over the mixture, forcing out the grounds which settle at the bottom of the pot.

French Roast—A very dark roast commonly used to make espresso. Dark brown to almost black in color, the beans appear shiny because of the oils that are "sweated" out during the roasting process. Low in acidity.

Full City Roast—A medium roast that is a darker brown than an American roast, though not as dark as an espresso roast. Full City is the darkest brown a bean can be roasted to without bringing out oils to the surface. It is a popular middle-of-the-road roast, used in many specialty coffee shops for making brewed coffee.

Granita—A drink made by freezing and then crushing espresso. Adding sugar keeps the frozen mixture granular rather than solid. To be eaten with a spoon.

Italian Roast—A very dark roast used for making espresso. The Italian roast results in a bean that is nearly black and shiny with the oils brought out during the roasting process. A Northern Italian roast is somewhat darker (the coffee is roasted a little longer), than a Southern Italian roast.

Latte—Similar to cappuccino but with much less foam and about three times as much steamed milk as espresso.

Latte Art—The creation of designs atop espresso drinks. The art work is a result of pouring velvety, microfoamed milk into designs such as rosettes, hearts, and fronds. Latte art can be performed only if all the steps in making the espresso drink are performed perfectly. Or, in the words of one barista, "If you do everything right, you can't not do latte art."

Lungo—Literally, a long shot of espresso, meaning the espresso is pulled for a longer time, yielding more than the standard 1–1¼-oz drink. There is more water than in a shorter shot, resulting in a thinner and lighter espresso. In short, longer is weaker.

Macchiato—An espresso topped with a dollop of frothed milk. In Italian, "macchiato" means "marked"—this drink is marked, or stained, by a drop of foam.

Mochaccino—A cappuccino to which chocolate syrup or powder has been added.

Organic—Organic coffee is grown without the use of pesticides. The term is often used to embrace all methods of soil and water conservation used in growing coffee that have a low impact on the environment. To be certified, a grower must produce its coffee for three consecutive years in accordance with standards set by a certifying agency approved by the US Department of Agriculture.

Portafilter—The handled filter basket on an espresso machine to which finely ground, compacted coffee is added. Available in different sizes for making single, double, and triple espressos.

Red Eye—A cup of brewed coffee to which a shot of espresso is added.

Ristretto—A short, or "restricted" shot of espresso, which is pulled for a shorter time, perhaps 20 seconds ("restricted" to the first, more flavorful, part of the pull), and results in a thicker, stronger drink slightly smaller than the standard one ounce. The opposite of a lungo.

Robusta—Coffee beans that come from the species of coffee tree called *coffea canephora*, one of the two major categories of coffee trees. Robustas, which are resistant to disease, are grown at lower altitudes than arabicas. With less flavor and twice as much caffeine as arabicas, they are used in instant coffees and supermarket-grade canned coffees. Still, many excellent espresso blends will include a bit of robusta to give added bite and to produce more crema.

Shade Grown—Coffee that is grown under a canopy of trees, rather than in full sun. The shade canopy provides a natural habitat for migratory birds, which explains why "shade-grown" is synonymous with "bird-friendly." The criteria for certifying coffee as shade grown come from the Rainforest Alliance.

Single Origin—Used synonymously with the term "varietal" to describe coffee that comes from a single geographic region—for example, Jamaica, Sumatra, Costa Rica, or Brazil—as opposed to a blend, which combines beans from different regions.

Specialty Coffee—Means different things to different people, but basically refers to coffee made with arabica beans from a micro-roaster and prepared in a coffee-centric, setting—that is, in a café by an experienced barista.

Sustainability—The notion of growing coffee in a way that has a low impact on (that is, sustains) the environment. Incorporates the commitment to minimizing pollution as well as the use of non-renewable resources. Eco-friendly.

Tamping—Compacting the coffee grounds in the portafilter of the espresso machine to regulate the flow of water through them. Best done with a tamper, a pestle-like device with a flat end, with about thirty pounds of pressure.

Vienna Roast—A dark brown roast, with a small amount of oils, roasted longer than a Full City but not as long as a French roast. Could be used for making espresso (it would be considered a very light espresso roast), or for brewed coffee, as Starbucks apparently does.